COPING WITH DIFFICULT PEOPLE
helps you:

- Identify six major types of difficult behavior

- Discover who is difficult—and why

- Master a step-by-step guide for coping

- Regain control of your life

COPING WITH DIFFICULT PEOPLE

Stop wishing they were different and learn how to deal with them!

"SOME OF THE SOLUTIONS WILL LEAVE YOU WONDERING, 'WHY DIDN'T I THINK OF THAT?' "
Tulsa World

Also by Robert M. Bramson, Ph. D.
Published by Ballantine Books:

THE STRESSLESS HOME

COPING WITH DIFFICULT PEOPLE

Robert M. Bramson, Ph.D.

BALLANTINE BOOKS • NEW YORK

To Susan, who paid for this book in many ways.

Library of Congress Catalog Card Number: 80-2319

ISBN 0-345-35294-7

This edition published by arrangement with
Anchor Press/Doubleday & Company, Inc.

Printed in Canada

First Ballantine Books Edition: October 1982
Fifteenth Printing: July 1987

CONTENTS

PREFACE

This book was written because I couldn't find another like it. How such ubiquitous phenomena as Difficult People had gone unnoticed and unexamined by any but acid wits and comic script writers is hard to fathom. Yet the gap existed and it needed to be, and could be, filled.

As a management consultant I have found that most of my clients spend more time talking about how to cope with problem employees, bosses, customers, and coworkers than about anything else. I have also found that there was much that I knew that could help these clients. Through observation and action research during a fourteen-year period, I and my associates had gathered practical information on techniques and methods for coping with Difficult People. It was the absence of any practical and integrated reference material, and repeated requests from the many people who attended our seminars, that set me on the long course of writing a book. I'm lucky that it also turned out to be fun.

The acknowledgments that need to be made are many. Fourteen years ago Stuart Atkins first piqued my curiosity about Difficult People with a presentation on six personality types that give salesmen trouble. I wondered if his six were indeed the most difficult and I decided to find out—they were. Stuart, Allan Katcher, and Elias Porter, Jr., enriched my own thoughts on interpersonal incompatibilities. The material on defensive behavior in Chapter 11 contains many of their ideas.

My partners, Nick Parlette, Allen F. Harrison, and Susan Bramson, have added much from their own experiences with clients and with Difficult People. They have also refined my understanding of why some methods work, and why others that ought to work, don't. Chapter 10 was written with Allen's kind assistance.

Wilson Yandell, more than any other person, deepened my understanding of the profound degree to which our own behavior is affected by our perceptions of what others intend toward us. Even more important, he showed me that freedom to move beyond the interaction of the moment depends upon seeing clearly the degree to which we affect and are affected by the expectations of others.

The sections on understanding the behavior of Difficult People in Chapters 2 to 8 contain my own integration of the views of a variety of authors, George Kelly more than others, supplemented by many interviews with the Difficult People themselves. They are not presented as definitive analytic explanations of what is very complex behavior. Rather, their purpose is to aid the reader to that "understanding from the inside," to use George Kelly's term, that gives freedom for constructive action to anyone caught up in a troublesome relationship.

Jonathan Cobb taught me much about writing as well as proposing many useful changes in the structure and flow of the manuscript. Similarly, Carol Mann, my agent, and my editor Marie Dutton Brown made valuable suggestions and provided much support.

To the many people who contributed data about themselves and the Difficult People in their lives, many thanks. It is they, not I, who have provided the substance of this book. Friends and neighbors may think that they see themselves in the examples used throughout the book—they are, however, mistaken.

My fond gratitude goes to Fred and Carolyn Batkin, who often allowed me to use their home as a hideaway.

Finally, my appreciation and love to Wendy, Don, Guinevere, Marni, Eric, Rob, Sean, Patrick, Jeremy, and Hillary for standing by me during the periods of cantankerous obsession or obliviousness that seem to be a necessary part of my writing a book.

Chapter 1

INTRODUCTION

This is a book about impossible people and how to cope with them. If your life is free from hostile customers and co-workers, indecisive, vacillating bosses, overagreeable (but do-nothing) subordinates or any of those others who deserve to be called Difficult People, read no further. Consider yourself extraordinarily lucky and move on to pleasanter fare. If, however, these constant headaches have intruded, read on, for the purpose of this book is to show you how to identify, understand, and cope with the Difficult People who come into your life. It is directed primarily at those who must work with others to accomplish common tasks, but the methods described here are applicable in many different settings. These methods have worked successfully for salespeople, customer-relations staff, engineers and scientists, bus drivers, teachers, psychiatry residents, probation, parole, and police officers, nurses, volunteers, high school students, and, of course, supervisors, managers and executives in both public and profit-making organizations.

Here are two of these Difficult People as seen by their victims. Frank, a dynamic assistant division chief in an aircraft manufacturing firm, was at his wits' end. This was the third opportunity he had missed to start a new project because George, his boss, through his indecisiveness, let it slip away. George had a reputation in the division for not being able to make important decisions. Frank was finding out why the hard way.

Frank liked George and respected his engineering abilities; that was partly what made their working relationship so exasperating. George could listen well, and he seemed to accept all of Frank's arguments. Then Frank would leave the office feeling great, only to wait for the memo from George that never was written. Frank felt he had tried everything: pushing his boss to come to a decision, leaving him alone for several weeks, cajol-

1

ing him, and arguing the selling points of the new project all over again. No matter what tactics he tried, he could not pry a response from George. Frank liked the firm and thought that he had a good chance for advancement, but the prospect of having to put up with George's indecisiveness indefinitely was depressing and frustrating.

"Art, I'll be honest with you. I've given up on Seth. I'm just going to cover my ass, lay low, and do my best to get rid of him." Nate was talking to Art, the vice-president of operations for Tetley Electronics, about his division head. Art was beginning to realize that no one in the design division of the company could stand Seth. Nate was the seventh employee in a month to complain about him. And it wasn't just the troublemakers and mediocre people who were complaining, either. Seth appeared to be making life in the division unpleasant for the competent and even the most easy-going. "He scolds the whole staff when one person is late for a meeting," Nate continued. "He bites your head off whenever you ask for help. He screams insults when he loses his temper, no matter who else is around. He won't listen when you try to explain anything. He's just impossible!"

George and Seth are what I call "Difficult People." We encounter people like them all the time. They are the hostile customers or co-workers, the indecisive, vacillating bosses, and the over-agreeable subordinates of the world who are constant headaches to work with. Although their numbers are small, their impact is large. They are responsible for absenteeism, significant losses in productivity, and lost customers or clients. They frustrate and demoralize those unlucky enough to have to work with them, and they are difficult to understand. Worst of all, they appear immune to all the usual methods of communication and persuasion designed to convince them or help them to change their ways.

Of course, we all can be hostile or over-agreeable or indecisive from time to time and be a drag on our associates, friends, and families. In this sense we are all, at times, "difficult." But there's an important difference between people like George and Seth and the rest of us. While each of us may occasionally thwart or annoy or confuse one or the other of our fellow creatures, a

Difficult Person's troublesome behavior is habitual and affects most of the people with whom he comes in contact. Difficult People are seen as problems by most of the people around them, not just those who are incompetent, overly sensitive, or weak.

The techniques for coping with the Difficult People whose descriptions make up the greater part of this book have been tried out and tested by many people who have found that they benefited in a number of ways by learning some techniques to apply in situations that formerly had left them fuming, yelling, or speechless. As a result they felt less angry and helpless in their encounters with the Difficult People in their lives, and, perhaps most significantly, they found that they were able to accomplish more, whether their Difficult People were bosses, peers, subordinates, clients, or customers.

HOW THE TECHNIQUES WERE DEVELOPED

For thirty years, I have worked in or with a variety of public and private organizations in positions ranging from blue-collar craftsman to manager. These experiences have left me with absolutely no doubt that there *are* Difficult People. When I then studied how people behave and learn at work, I searched for ways of understanding how they came to be that way. As a management consultant, I discovered that they could be coped with effectively.

For fourteen years now, my associates and I have observed, questioned, and listened as executives and staff members working in more than two hundred diverse organizations told us about the most troublesome people in their working lives. Our primary objective in this investigation was to increase our own ability to help our clients work more effectively with or minimize discord caused by their own problem people. In the early stages of this investigation, we verified that there were indeed similarities in difficult behavior. Over a four-year period we asked several hundred men and women to talk about the most Difficult People in their lives. We found that the same kinds of behavior patterns were identified over and over again, some considerably more than others. Later our attention turned to what could be done about the behavior. These findings, subsequently refined and elaborated upon, form the basis for a part of my present consulting program and the substance of this book.

PATTERNS OF DIFFICULT BEHAVIOR

The behavior patterns that seem to be the most disruptive or frustrating are characterized by the following types.

Hostile-Aggressives: These are the people who, like Seth, try to bully and overwhelm by bombarding others, making cutting remarks, or throwing tantrums when things don't go the way they are certain things should.

Complainers: Complainers are individuals who gripe incessantly but who never try to do anything about what they complain about, either because they feel powerless to do so or because they refuse to bear the responsibility.

Silent and Unresponsives: These are the people who respond to every question you might have, every plea for help you make, with a yep, a no, or a grunt.

Super-Agreeables: Often very personable, funny, and outgoing individuals, Super-Agreeables are always very reasonable, sincere, and supportive in your presence but don't produce what they say they will, or act contrary to the way they have led you to expect.

Negativists: When a project is proposed, the Negativists are bound to object with "It won't work" or "It's impossible." All too often they effectively deflate any optimism you might have.

Know-It-All Experts: These are those "superior" people who believe, and want you to recognize, that they know everything there is to know about anything worth knowing. They're condescending, imposing (if they really do know what they're talking about), or pompous (if they don't), and they will likely make you feel like an idiot.

Indecisives: Those who stall major decisions until the decision is made for them (like George), those who can't let go of anything until it is perfect—which means never.

Although Complainers don't always complain, and Indecisives sometimes do make decisions, there are common patterns in the behavior of Difficult People that can be identified and described. As you will see, finding and labeling these patterns helps set the stage for taking effective action.

THE NATURE OF COPING

While identifying Difficult People in work settings was useful, we came to an even more fascinating realization during our observations. In many of the work groups observed, there were one or two individuals who could deal reasonably well with the same Seths and Georges who had stumped their colleagues. Those who coped well with each type of Difficult Person used similar methods that could be identified and learned. What did these "copers" do? What did they avoid doing? Most importantly, how might the methods they used be communicated to others? The answers to these questions make up the core of this book.

What, precisely, then, is "coping"? According to the standard definitions, *coping* means "to contend on equal terms," exactly what one needs to do with Difficult People. Individuals behave in a difficult manner because they have learned that doing so keeps others off balance and incapable of effective action. Whether brow-beating others into acquiescence or avoiding distress by sitting on a decision, Difficult People manage to gain control over others. That they are often not motivated to manipulate others and that they are largely unaware of the long-term costs of what they do is incidental to the fact that they put you at a disadvantage.

Effective coping, the term we will use in this book, is the sum of those actions that you can take to right the power balance, to minimize the impact of others' difficult behavior in the immediate situation in which you find yourself.

The refreshing thing about coping as an approach is that it provides an alternative to both "acceptance" ("She doesn't have much of a family life, so I try to overlook her lousy behavior") and to long, costly efforts to change that collection of attitudes, values, and learned strategies that we call personality ("Nothing's going to help him but three years on the couch"). Acceptance, while it avoids the unpleasantness of confrontation, is attained at a double cost to the individual coper—a feeling of martyrdom in the accepter and reinforcement of the behavior hated in the Difficult Person. Trying to change another person's personality, on the other hand, can be the world's greatest hard luck story. Not that it wouldn't be nice to change Difficult People; it surely would. Even when an individual has chosen to change, however, the way is difficult and expensive in terms of time, effort, and money. When the motivation for change comes primarily from outside the person—from supervisors, for example—it is even more costly and much less likely to work.

Coping, by contrast, has a much more limited and practical goal. Coping enables you *and* the Difficult Person to get on with the business at hand. Coping methods work because they interfere with the "successful" functioning of difficult behavior. When the behavior strategies of the Difficult Person don't work, when you respond in ways different from those expected, you are able to get about your business and the Difficult Person is provided with an incentive, and an opportunity, to develop other, more constructive behavior.

This approach to dealing with Difficult People does require that you act with purpose and with forethought in relating to them. In that sense, it is open to the charge of being manipulative. But I would contend that it nevertheless can be highly ethical. What makes purposive behavior ethical or evil is the *intention* of the doer. The coping methods described in this book are not designed to use people's motives against them, or to be sneaky or underhanded. They do not require that your intentions, and the actions you take to implement those intentions, be designed to further your own interests at the other person's expense. Their intended purpose, rather, is to balance the power Difficult People can have over you, and to further your mutual interests by producing a situation in which you both can function as productively as possible.

THE PLAN OF THE BOOK

In the pages that follow we will discuss methods for coping with difficult behavior and how to put them into practice. In Chapters 2 through 8, we will examine the seven difficult-behavior types who at least in work settings are the most irritating, frustrating, or overwhelming: Hostile-Aggressives, Complainers, Silent and Unresponsives, Super-Agreeables, Know-It-All Experts, Negativists, and Indecisives. In each of these chapters we will discuss how to recognize the behavior, how to understand why Difficult People persist in their discordant ways, and how to cope effectively with them.

Chapter 9 provides an overview of the coping process. It explains six basic steps to take in coping with just about anyone. It then takes you through a series of questions that help you analyze your relationship with potentially difficult others, leading to an action plan for coping with them. Use this chapter to help you distinguish between those whose difficult behavior is transitory and those with whom it has become a preferred way of dealing with life.

Chapter 10 provides some theory for those who are interested, outlining a framework for understanding the fascinating, if ironic, relationship between any person's positive and negative behavior. Not only does this understanding help to see Difficult People as they are, not as you wish them to be, but it provides a basis for preventing difficult behavior.

Building upon Chapter 10, Chapter 11 provides steps for keeping yourself in hand in the face of a Difficult Person's onslaught, with some special notes on dealing with your boss. It ends with a series of questions that will help you develop a plan for coping with a Difficult Person who might be currently intruding on your own life.

These chapters constitute a tactical manual of methods for coping with the Difficult People you are most likely to find troublesome.

The summaries that follow each section provide a quick reminder device to review just before you expect an encounter with a particular Difficult Person.

Coping with the Difficult People in your life will never be enjoyable. But this book provides the means for doing it with more ease and greater success.

Chapter 2

A HOSTILE-AGGRESSIVE TRIO: SHERMAN TANKS, SNIPERS, AND EXPLODERS

CASE #1: "I'm really sorry, Mr. Beales," said the assistant to the advertising director, "but Mr. Hart isn't here today. He left an hour ago for Chicago."

"What do you mean he isn't here?" said Beales, an important customer. "Goddamn it, I flew two hundred miles to see him and you tell me he isn't here? How could you make such a dumb mistake?"

"Well," said the assistant, "I've checked Mr. Hart's calendar and you're down for next week. I'm sure that . . ."

"Oh, for Christ's sake, stop lying and making excuses. What are you going to do about this? Damn it, answer me!"

"I don't really know what . . ." tried the assistant.

"What's your name?" Beales shouted. "The president of this company is a friend of mine, and I'm going to let him know what incompetents he has working for him."

The assistant stood staring blankly at Mr. Beales. Finally he pulled out his card, handed it over, and watched as Beales stamped out of the office.

"That loudmouth!" the assistant said to Mr. Hart's secretary. "He didn't wait long enough for me to tell him that I might catch Hart before his plane leaves."

"Well," said the secretary, "you didn't try too hard to tell him."

"Would you have?" mumbled the assistant as he mechanically walked back to his office, enraged at Beales for having chopped him down but worried too about whether he'd still have his job next week.

CASE #2: My client Charlie, division manager for a large and growing company, and I were reviewing what

had happened since the last time I had met with him and
his management team. Suddenly, he pushed away from
the table and said: "This is just a waste of time. I can't
concentrate on anything you're saying. Anyway, it doesn't
matter—I'm going to quit." In two weeks, Charlie proceeded to tell me, he was supposed to present to an
executive committee meeting a plan for a comprehensive
and expensive project that he had developed over the past
two years. "I can tell you just what would happen if I
went to the meeting. It's Leonard the Louse, our executive vice-president. That son of a bitch is going to kill
me, just as he's done three times in the past. He's mean,
he's sarcastic, he seems actually to enjoy cutting people
down. He'll ridicule me in front of those important
people, there'll be no approval, and I'll leave feeling like
a nothing. Even Jerry, my boss, a VP himself, is scared
to death of Leonard. I can't take it any longer. I'd rather
quit than be humiliated by him again."

Mr. Beales and Leonard the Louse well represent that
corrosive Difficult Person, the Hostile-Aggressive, most
often cited as the nemesis of those in the working world,
and these scenes illustrate their disruptive impact on an
average work day. As the name implies, they combine
an active, moving-out aggressiveness with hostility in a
fearsome way. Hostility and aggression appear together
so much it's easy to think of them as either inseparable
or interchangeable, but they are not; it is possible to be
aggressive without being hostile and vice versa. Aggressiveness is that quality we see in people who attempt
to shape the world as they want it to be or believe it
ought to be. A person can be highly aggressive yet caring:
"You're having trouble and you need help. I'm here to
see that you get it and use it, even if I have to push you
into doing what's good for you." Similarly, hostility, contentious and intending to wound, can be coupled with an
absence of direct aggression. That silent unresponsive person who refuses to respond to your desire or need for
conversation may be expressing hostility, for instance.

In this chapter we will examine three different ways in
which the qualities of hostility and aggressiveness combine into very abrasive behavior, and specific methods
for coping with each of them. I've named them the
Sherman Tank, the Sniper, and the Exploder.

THE SHERMAN TANK

The term *Sherman Tank* comes from a phrase a friend of mine used in describing a work associate who fitted this category perfectly:

> I've never seen such a person before, and I hope I never do again. If I did anything at all that didn't come up to her notions of how it should be done, she would walk over to where I was working, stand over me, and say things like, "Here's the brain of all brains. How can you keep doing things wrong when even an idiot would know the right thing to do?" Once she dropped a book right in the middle of my desk, spilling coffee, and leaving me so angry that I burst into tears. I knew that I shouldn't let her treat me that way, but while she was standing there yelling at me, I felt as if I were being run over by a Sherman Tank.

THE BEHAVIOR

Sherman Tanks come out charging, not always physically perhaps, but their whole demeanor expresses "attack." They are like my friend's nemesis—abusive, abrupt, intimidating, and, most important, overwhelming. They are arbitrary and often arrogant in tone. When criticizing something you've said or done, they seem to attack not just the particular behavior but *you*, and they do so in an accusing way. They are contemptuous of their victims, considering them to be inferior people who deserve to be bullied and disparaged.

Some persons who fit this mold attack crudely, with vulgarity that is itself distressing. Others are skillful enough to produce the Sherman Tank effect not by bitter tirade but by unrelenting criticism and argument that pushes others to acquiesce against their own best judgement. In many situations it is difficult to differentiate between useful persistance and overbearing, railroading behavior. That is why Sherman Tanks who have developed a modicum of smoothness often have been able to attain positions of authority and power. Having learned to attack and to follow through as well, Sherman Tanks possess tremendous power in interpersonal situations. Such power comes largely from the typical responses their behavior arouses:

confusion, mental or physical flight, or a sense of helpless frustration that leads to tears or tantrumlike rage.

Here is how some of the victims have described their feelings of loss of self-possession: "I felt confused, frightened—I couldn't get a word in—no time to think." "My heart was beating like a drum—I thought she was going to kill me." "I lost control of myself. I could feel the veins pounding in my head and I just wanted to shut his mouth." "I was so furious that I threw the door open, making a dent in the wall."

While these reactions are understandable, they rob the victim of the ability to deal coolly and competently with the situation at hand. Through this vacuum of cool competence the Sherman Tank proceeds. Evidence of rage or weakness, far from slowing down the Sherman Tank, often stimulates him or her to push on. To understand why these typical responses to the assaults of Sherman Tanks are apt to encourage rather than deter them and to discover what will work, we need to first know more about what underlies the Sherman Tank behavior.

UNDERSTANDING SHERMAN TANKS

Sherman Tanks have strong needs to prove to themselves, and others, that their view of the world is always right. Tasks to be done seem clear and concrete to them, and the way to perform them straightforward and simple. They get impatient with those who don't see what to them is plainly there. When resistance to their own plans is perceived or anticipated, impatience turns quickly to irritation, righteous indignation, or outright anger.

Sherman Tanks have a strong sense of what others *should* do; this quality is coupled with the forcefulness and supreme confidence that stem from the very fact that they have done so well at pulverizing others. Sadly—for others, that is—Tanks seem to lack the leavening of caring and trust that in most of us prevent the overuse of aggression.

Sherman Tanks usually achieve their short-run objectives, but they do so at the cost of honest disagreement from others, lost friendships, and the long-term erosion of relationships with their co-workers. Those people who are abrasive enough to be called "difficult" seem to lack the capacity to receive and accept feedback about their impact on others. They lack that critical discernment which helps to differentiate those situations which might indeed call for an overwhelming attack from those which should receive much less force.

Because Sherman Tanks value aggressiveness and confidence, they tend to devalue those they believe lack these qualities. Unfortunately, demeaning others is one way to create a sense of self-importance and superiority. If I can make you out to be weak, faltering, or equivocal, then I will seem, to myself and to others, strong and sure. That is the learned rule-of-thumb that sits in the back of the Sherman Tank's mind. It is, of course, to some extent true. That is why it was learned and reinforced.

Sherman Tanks, then, are driven by a need to demonstrate that they are right. They feel righteous anger toward those who do not do as they "should," which justifies hurting them. Finally, they expect others to run from them, and devalue them when they do.

HOW TO COPE WITH SHERMAN TANKS

Coping with Sherman Tanks requires that you not fulfill their expectation that, through either fear or rage, you will be put out of commission; at the same time you must avoid an open confrontation with them over who is right or who is to be the winner. Here are the specific things to do, and not do.

Stand Up for Yourself.

The first rule of coping with anyone aggressive, hostile or not, is that you *stand up* to that person. If you let yourself be pushed around by aggressive people, you simply fade into the scenery for them. That is, they will not see you as someone to whom attention need be paid. The next time you are with a group in which something important is being discussed, watch for the following kind of situation. Mark raises an idea for consideration only to have Sharon, an aggressive person, say something like, "No! No, that won't work at all." Unless Mark does something to stand up for himself, such as saying, "Well, wait a minute, I'm not sure you really heard what I was trying to say," something very interesting will happen. Sharon will begin to act as if Mark is not a part of the meeting. She won't look at him, she will speak through him, she will not react to anything that he says.

You must, therefore, stand up to any sort of aggressive person to ensure that you make genuine and solid contact with him or her. There is always the possibility that the individual whom you think is a Sherman Tank may be just a nonhostile, but aggressive, person trying to get at the facts and not at you. If you don't stand up, then you will feel unnecessarily overrun, and he or she will feel frustrated.

Important rules for coping with aggressive people in general are doubly important when encountering a Sherman Tank. Your acquiescence will be taken not simply as a sign that you're not worth bothering about but as a license to squash you. True, when you are being overwhelmed by a Sherman Tank the last thing you are likely to want to do is stand up to him or her, particularly when the assault is coming from a person who has real authority over you. The sense of being overwhelmed evokes, in most people, images of overpowering, possibly physically aggressive, and accusing parents. Perhaps this explains the frequency with which the victims of Sherman Tank behavior tend to recall such incidents as if *they* were the difficult ones. In coping with these very Difficult People, it helps to recognize that the fear and confusion that you feel are natural, even appropriate reactions to being attacked. Expect to feel distraught, angry, or awkward, but say something of a standing up nature anyway. The following pointers may help.

Give Them Time to Run Down.

If the person you are confronting is yelling at you, crying angrily, or being otherwise noisy, hold your position for a short while to give them time to run down. Remain in place (unless you need to move to guard against physical assault), look directly at the yeller, and wait. When the Sherman Tank's attack begins to lose momentum, jump into the situation.

Don't Worry About Being Polite, Just Get In.

If you wait for a Hostile-Aggressive to finish sentences and conscientiously give you time to enter the conversation, you are likely to wait a long time. It is often necessary to interrupt in order to stand up to him or her. This is a time when cutting people off before they're through is a necessity. If you, in turn, are cut off before you've finished your thought, say firmly and loudly, "You interrupted me!" If the Tank doesn't stop, say it again. Then start in yourself. Don't worry about how well you express it. Smile if you have to, but say it.

Get Their Attention, Carefully.

Sherman Tanks tend to have firm expectations of how you are going to react to them. After all, why should you be different from all their previous victims? You need, therefore, to get their attention so that they recognize that you won't be responding according to their formula —that is, by either running or raging.

For this reason, I have found that it often helps to begin coping efforts by clearly and loudly calling the hostile person by name (by his or her name, that is, not *a* name). Use the name that fits the present level of your acquaintance. Don't, for instance, call that customer Sally as a way of diminishing her status, if you would ordinarily call her Mrs. Harrison.

Other ways of both getting attention and interrupting the interaction are rising very deliberately or dropping a book or a pencil. You should be careful, however, that your moves can't be interpreted as a sharp or sudden attack. For example, be sure that while standing up, you take pains to push your chair backwards. Picture it. If you don't do this, the upper part of your body will propel forward into what can seem to be a fighting stance.

Get Them to Sit Down.

If at all possible, try to get your Sherman Tank into a seated position. Since most people behave less aggressively when seated, it's worth a try. Point to a chair and say, "Look, if we're going to argue we might as well be comfortable." Start to sit down yourself, *but* keep your eye on the Tank. If he or she doesn't sit, remain standing yourself. Having a Tank standing accusingly over you does not make coping easier.

Speak from Your Own Point of View.

Certain words and phrases project a self-assertive quality. They clearly express your own viewpoint or perception, yet do not imply a direct attack on anything the other person has said. Examples of such words and phrases are: "In my opinion, it's a good idea . . ."; "I disagree with you . . ." (or if it's your boss, "I guess I disagree with you . . ."); "I can see that you don't think much of him as a teacher, but my experience with him has been different." By using phrases like these, you have not told the other person what to do, how to feel or think, or even that he or she is wrong. You are instead signaling that you are expressing your own views, feelings, or perceptions about whatever is being considered.

Avoid a Head-On Fight.

Given the value of not retreating before a Sherman Tank's onslaught, why is it so important to avoid fighting to win? There are basically two reasons, one connected with short-term and the other with long-term risks.

1) *You may lose the battle.* When you fight, your efforts are directed toward prevailing, winning, forcing "them" to back down. However, the Sherman Tank type of Hostile-Aggressive just cannot give in. Tanks will react to your combative behavior with an escalation of their own assault. When that happens, you are apt to be sorry, because you are likely to lose.

Sherman Tanks tend to be good at fighting; they usually have been perfecting their skills for a long time, and they have found it a powerful way to deal with other people. You, on the other hand, unless you are also highly aggressive, are an amateur. You are not so motivated by a deeply ingrained need to validate your own version of reality. You also probably do not have at hand the weaponry of carefully refined cutting phrases or freely flung profanity.

When you fight with a Sherman Tank whose power frightens you, you may be tempted to do it by taking pot shots at him or her, or what we'll call "sniping" later in the chapter. I do not know of a surer way to get blasted, however. Sherman Tanks are unlikely to hold back a counterattack just because they don't want to cause a fuss.

Furthermore, the very fact that Sherman Tanks have *had* successes in fighting will keep them in the field longer than most others. In other words, they will persist whereas you likely will not. They will at least persist long enough for you to withdraw from the action or give in, as your initial anger dries up and you need your own early learned urgings toward restraint.

2) *You may win the battle but lose the war.* Even if *you* are an aggressive person and a skillful fighter, there are good reasons for learning to use that strength to stand up to Sherman Tanks rather than fight with them. Primary among these is the fact that when the person you are fighting is your boss (or for that matter your spouse or your child), you will be the eventual loser, even if you win the immediate encounter. Being defeated and overwhelmed does not cure Hostile-Aggressives. Instead it leaves them seething and plotting, driven underground as Snipers, or disoriented, highly anxious, and perhaps dangerous. Imagine what your situation would be if, instead of standing up to a Sherman Tank boss, you cut down, out-shouted, and forced him or her to back off. How will your budget requests fare in the future? What will your chances for promotion be? You may gain a tremendous feeling of satisfaction at having gotten even, but you may be trading that off against your career, inviting anxiety over the potential revenge of the Sherman Tank, and missing the satisfaction of being able to cope in a way that will make you and your adversary more productive.

A second reason for not fighting, even if you can win, is the possible impression you will make on observers of such a battle. If you chop down a Hostile-Aggressive co-worker, you may be seen by people of importance to you simply as a brawler rather than a hero. In other words, you will have accrued some of the same negative feelings toward you as the Sherman Tank and your relationships will suffer accordingly.

Be Ready to be Friendly.

Hostile-Aggressives, when they have been stood up to but not personally defeated, may make friendly overtures to you. This curious turn of events has long been recognized in folk wisdom as "stand up to the bully and he'll become your friend." Perhaps the change occurs because the Sherman Tank, not having been able to overwhelm you, yet not feeling that you are a competitor, sees you now as worthy of respect. Or perhaps the shift takes place because of a deep need for acceptance among Sherman Tanks that can only be expressed to someone who is strong. Whatever the reasons for it, the feelings are usually genuine.

If you are not ready for this to happen, you may react with anger that will get in the way of a productive and valuable future relationship.

COPING IN PRACTICE

Let's now see what this coping strategy looks like in an actual situation and then consider how you can implement it when the Sherman Tank is in a position of considerable authority over you.

Back at the Meeting.

At the beginning of this chapter, I described the problem that my client, Charlie, faced with Leonard, his executive vice-president. Charlie expected that Leonard would chop him down in front of the most important people in the company, as he had several times in the past.

Charlie and I talked for a while about Leonard, and I outlined to him the techniques for coping with skillful Sherman Tanks such as Leonard. Charlie wryly said that since he was going to quit anyway, he might as well try. Later that week we worked together for another hour; with my coaching and considerable support, he practiced just what he would do if the meeting turned out as he feared.

Charlie obtained permission for me to attend the meeting as a consultant for his project, and on the appointed day we entered the conference room a little early to give him time to set up and pass around the thick data books his staff had prepared. At 1:30 he began his presentation.

For the first twenty minutes, Leonard did everything a Sherman Tank, barely under wraps, might be expected to do. He appeared not to be listening, moved around in his chair, and thumbed idly through the papers, making his inattentiveness plain to everyone in the room.

About a third of the way through Charlie's presentation, Leonard showed that he well merited his reputation. He stood up, turned his back on my client and eyed his fellow vice-presidents. He cut Charlie off in midsentence, saying, "All right, I'm tired of listening to this crap! This is the stupidest thing I've ever heard of. Why do we have to be subjected to this guy and another of his idiotic, magnificent schemes? What's next on the agenda?" The tone was disdainful, the sarcasm biting, and the following silence thick enough to slice.

Charlie sat down in shock and struggled to get hold of himself. The president, a very sweet guy who had hired Leonard to complement his own indecisiveness, turned to my client and mumbled, "Well, Charlie, uh . . . thank you for coming in. We'll talk it over and then we'll let you know." Here is where Charlie moved back in, coped, and changed his relationship with Leonard. He stood up, interrupted the president, and turned to face Leonard, who had walked away from the table and was looking out a window. In a loud and rather tense voice, Charlie said, "Leonard, at this point I can see you don't think our proposal is any good—I hear that. But I disagree with you. In my judgment, this is a good proposal. I think it's important. I believe it's going to help with some problems that our company is bound to run into over the next five years. What I expect from you right now is that you'll sit down and listen while I finish going through the proposal. Then we can talk about whether it's any good or not."

Without waiting for anyone's permission, Charlie then calmly (on the outside, that is) walked back to the easel and pushed on with his proposal. (He later said that he felt "just like Humphrey Bogart" at this point.) Leonard walked back to the table and looked at my client as if he had never seen him before, as he likely had not. He stood in back of his chair for a moment, then threw an angrily challenging question at Charlie who fielded it well with "I'll get to that in a minute, Leonard." After a bit he sat down, listened intently to the presentation, and then rapidly began flipping through the written back-up material. My guess was that, as is often characteristic of highly aggressive people, he had barely listened at the beginning before concluding that the project was "idiotic." He now needed to catch up. Soon, however, he interrupted Charlie with a number of pointed, intelligent, and insightful questions. I judged him to be a highly capable individual who had risen to his high position through a combination of intelligence and a neat ability to run over others.

The meeting went on until early evening. In the end, the executive committee voted to give Charlie half of the money he had requested. Two aspects of the decision are noteworthy. First, they concluded the discussion right there, while Charlie was in the room, rather than following the usual practice of politely dismissing him while they decided on a response. Second, although the executive committee only budgeted half of what was asked for, they did *not* do it as a kind of reluctant compromise, voting a skimpy budget for the entire project. Instead, they funded the project fully during the first phase of operation, with the proviso that if it appeared to live up to its promise, the committee would allocate enough to carry it through until it would be self-supporting.

When the discussion finally ended, everyone was played out, perhaps feeling satisfied, but drained. It was at this point that Leonard bounced up with a big smile on his face. He walked around the table, stood about three feet away from Charlie and, with his index finger pointed straight at him, said, "Charlie, you mean bastard, let's go have a drink." Then he put his arm around Charlie's shoulders and walked him to the coat rack and on out the door.

Charlie said to me later, "It's a good thing you told me about Hostile-Aggressive people wanting to be friendly, because when he put his arm around me, the skin on my shoulders began to crawl. Going through my mind was, 'For two years you put me through hell, and now you want to go out and have a drink.' What I really wanted to do was let fly with my elbow right into his side. But, as you know, I went out with him. The hell of it is— he turned out to be a very nice guy." My client did not resign.

Can You Really Kill Giants?

What are the odds that these methods will work against someone much more powerful than you, a high government official, a big boss in your company, or an important faculty member? I believe the odds are quite good, but naturally the strategy must be executed with particular care. In these situations, it is especially important to plan in advance and to have fall-back positions in mind. The most important of these is a clear and unambiguous statement that your intention was not to rebel against the boss's authority: "Wait a minute, if you think that I don't know that you're in charge, you're wrong. You're the boss! Whatever you finally decide, I'll do my best. But I do have some ideas on what our policy should be."

That people can refuse to allow themselves to be demeaned by Sherman Tanks in positions of authority over them and still keep their jobs is not a fairy story—it has been demonstrated to me many times. Standing up to Sherman Tanks in the way I've described seems to work even when carried out in an uncertain, somewhat timid manner. This was brought home to me by a letter from a rather quiet, middle-aged woman who had retrained herself as a secretary after fifteen years in retail selling.

Just after I had started working as a secretary, my boss, in an abusive and sarcastic way, told me that she was sorry that she had hired me. She told me about three mistakes that I had made in preparing a report for her signature and ended the conversation with, "Do it again! Maybe this time even *you'll* get it right." My boss was a very important executive in the company. At that time, I really didn't want to lose the job and wasn't sure what to do, so I went ahead and corrected the report and meekly gave it back to her.

About ten days later she came out to my desk and began shouting about the whereabouts of two letters that she needed to take up to the President's office. She yelled at me and told me to "jump." At that point I was unable to respond, but two days later I called her on the intercom and asked for (and got) an appointment for that afternoon at 3:00. I was so nervous that I wrote out what I wanted to say to her and read it off my paper. I told her that I liked the job, wanted to keep it, and thought that she was doing very important work, but that I couldn't let her speak to me the way she had. "You have a right to say anything you want to about my work," I said, "but you don't have a right to make me feel that I don't amount to anything at all." She just sat there and then asked me if I had anything more to say. I said no, and left the office feeling that my job was gone. She never did say anything at all about our conversation. However, after that she did not yell at me, although I must say that she did yell about other people in my presence.

Before you take on one of these "heavies," here are some points to consider.

Can this person injure you secretly? For example, is he or she an owner who can fire you without anyone else's approval? In contrast, will vindictiveness on his or her part always be visible to others, the personnel director, for example? It is unlikely that any executive will get much sympathy for saying, "I want to fire that person (you) because she objects to my insulting her."

Is your own work up to standard? You don't want to charge and then find that your rear is exposed.

Can you distinguish negative criticism of your work or on-the-job behavior, legitimate even if you don't like it, from a personal attack on you? This is the very distinction that needs to be made when you stand up to the person who is running roughshod over you.

REVIEW OF COPING WITH SHERMAN TANKS

To cope with Sherman Tanks you must stand up to them without fighting.

—Give them a little time to run down.
—Don't worry about being polite; get in any way you can.
—Get their attention, perhaps by calling them by name or sitting or standing deliberately.
—If possible, get them to sit down.
—Maintain eye contact.
—State your own opinions and perceptions forcefully.
—Don't argue with what the other person says or try to cut him or her down.
—Be ready to be friendly.

The basic principle of standing up to someone without fighting lies behind successful coping with all Hostile-Aggressive people. In the case of the Sniper, second of the three Hostile-Aggressive cousins we are discussing in this chapter, this principle should be applied in a way quite different from that used with Sherman Tanks, however; we'll see why in the next section.

THE SNIPER

One of the clearest sketches of a Sniper was provided by Millie, a thoughtful and perceptive financial analyst in a brokerage firm. She described the Sniper in her group this way

> I inwardly groan when we have an analyst planning meeting. Burt, really a pretty good analyst, seems to enjoy undercutting Stan, our manager. No matter what Stan does, Burt can always think of something negative to say about him. For example, when Stan is putting something up on a flip chart, Burt will whisper to the rest of us, "How can one man be so dull?" When Stan got his big promotion, and we all went over to celebrate, Burt spent the evening saying things like, "I wonder how soon they'll find out about him this time."
>
> But it's not only what Burt says, it's that he always covers it with a big smile or a laugh. He'll even get smiles back from other people, even though they've told me later that they feel cowardly in doing it. I think it would be better if Burt would be openly critical of Stan. It's the way he does it—by making a thumbs down gesture when Stan has said something that the rest of us thought was pretty good, and things like that —that bothers me so much.

THE BEHAVIOR

Snipers do not come crashing down on you. They maintain a cover, if often thin or transparent, from behind which they take pot shots at you. Their weapons are rocks hidden in snowballs: innuendos, *sotto voce* remarks, not-too-subtle digs, nonplayful teasing, and the like. As we have seen, when confronted by a Sherman Tank's open assault, the common reaction is either to run or fight back. In the face of the covert attack by the Sniper, however, feelings of being completely pinned down are the most characteristic, as if there were no response choices at all. The chosen recipients are struck by well-placed verbal missiles, high-powered enough to hurt.

But the attack is accompanied by nonverbal signals that say "Pretend that what I'm doing is nice or neutral, or that you don't even hear me."

Bystanders, like Millie, who have watched a Burt in action, often later describe an angry wish that the victim make some kind of deliberate and open response—return the insult, yell, or simply haul off and hit the aggressor. Yet that is just what the victim is unlikely to do, even when he or she is otherwise strong and active. Whether the person being attacked is supervisor, subordinate, husband, wife, or teacher, the skillful Sniper has learned to use the rituals and social constraints in which the victims participate to create a protected place from which to strike out at objects of anger or envy.

I am often amazed at the length of time that bosses, not to mention parents, will tolerate a Sniper in their midst, even though they complain about the cost to themselves and other group members. It is this very success in reducing others to inaction that is so reinforcing to the Sniper. And yet, once again, there is a certain sad and self-defeating cost to this slick if nasty form of attack. Even from the Sniper's point of view, paralysis of action hardly represents any real solutions to problems at hand. Snipers certainly generate in others the same kind of inner resentment that Sherman Tanks do, yet they do not gain the compensating power to move others to action. At whatever long-run cost, Charlie's assailant completely dominated the situation. Burt only succeeded in demotivating his boss, weakening his ability to provide effective leadership.

The cycle is a sad one. Sniping behavior is often a response to an unresolved or unheeded problem. However, while it causes much distress, sniping hardly ever results in positive action. The unresolved problems continue or become worse, and the resulting stress produces more difficult behavior. This self-destructive cycle will continue until the victim decides to stop being a victim, thus changing the nature of the interaction.

UNDERSTANDING THE BEHAVIOR

Snipers have in common with Sherman Tanks a very strong sense of how others ought to think and act. They often have firm views of what can be done to solve the problems that interfere with their own personal goals. However, since their "I'm superior" orientation tends to interfere with seeing things from others' perspectives, what Snipers expect from a boss, co-workers, or spouse is often unrealistic.

It is common in both large and small organizations for a worker to expect his or her immediate boss to be able to make changes in overall policy over which the boss has no say. In a corporation that makes farm machinery, for example, when the decision came down that the line of cultivators was to be marked up 30 percent, the sales manager, who felt that the rise would lead to a dramatic drop in sales, unrealistically expected his immediate superior to get the price lowered. However, unrealistic or not, when Snipers' expectations are not met, their strong motivation to get their way may lead to more frequent and more cutting attacks. Not, regretfully, on the problems, but on those "objects" who need to be punished, or covertly pushed into doing the "right" things. That sniping sales manager just mentioned began to mention at every available opportunity, in his boss's presence, of course, that it certainly took a lot of gumption to tell one's superior the truth about matters, the implication, of course, being that his own boss was weak and cowardly.

That the overuse of aggression comes out as Sniping rather than Sherman Tanking is probably due to elements in the immediate situation. Aggressive people like to win or, more accurately, they don't like losing. They particularly don't like feeling that they are not in some way in control of the situation. However, when those with whom they must contend have the power to reward or punish, it is not practical to risk a battle, especially when there is another, less dangerous way. The Sniper maxim is: If I undercut you and make you look ridiculous, I can reaffirm the rightness of my own view of things without the danger of being overwhelmed myself. Most importantly, I can still feel in control of the situation.

I suspect that an even more basic reason Snipers choose a hidden rather than a frontal attack is simply that they have developed the skill with which to do it. Using a dart to kill requires more skill than using a bludgeon. I have seen many crude and inept Sherman Tanks, but few such Snipers. Unsubtle Snipers usually meet the fate of their unskillful wartime counterparts: quickly discovered, they are even more quickly shot out of the trees.

It is useful to remember, however, that Snipers and Sherman Tanks *are* close cousins under the skin. Covert Hostile-Aggressive people can come out shouting when the situational restrictions have been removed or when their cover has been penetrated. It helps to keep this in mind when coping with a Sniper. You can shift to Sherman Tank coping steps much more effectively if you are prepared for your adversary's change of style.

COPING METHODS

The Sniper's cover, as we have seen, is constructed inadvertently by his or her victims, out of their devotion to a mix of social conventions and a common distaste for causing scenes. Therefore, as with the emperor's new clothes, the cover disappears when the true circumstances are described.

Keep in mind that your main purpose is getting on with your business—coping—rather than changing or punishing. The method of choice is one that will not force out the potential Sherman Tank that lies within the Sniper, but instead one that will provide a path for a more constructive use of the carping and critical perspective of the Sniper. The coping steps for doing this are these: (1) surface the attack; (2) provide a peaceful alternative to open warfare; (3) seek group confirmation or denial of the Sniper's criticism; (4) deal with the underlying problems.

Surface the Attack.

The first thing to do with Snipers is to smoke them out. If you are the target yourself, refuse to be attacked indirectly. Ask questions like: "That sounded like a dig, did you mean it that way?" "What did you mean when you turned your thumbs down while I was telling my story?" If the put-down occurs during a presentation you are giving, stop, turn to the Sniper, and say: "Do I understand that you don't like what I'm saying?" If your Sniper responds by ridiculing you further, put words to that, too: "Sounds like you're ridiculing me, are you?"

Expect that your impulse will be to ignore or laugh off the barb. Your sense of politeness and self-expectation will urge you to go along with the masquerade and, at all costs, not be disruptive. Use any behavioral props you need to get over this barrier: smile, raise your eyebrows, act coy, or whatever. But do say something that will not let the slight go by unremarked.

Provide the Sniper an Alternative to a Direct Contest.

You'll note that all of the examples of responses I've given are phrased as questions rather than assertions. The reason for this is that the question format gives the Sniper an alternative to fighting. Usually the Sniper will flatly deny an attack was intended. "Who me? Oh, no, I agree with what you're saying." The fact that you have successfully stood up to the attack, weathered it, yet not escalated it will help you to proceed with your coping. Even if your Sniper has denied everything and you have accepted the denial, he or she will be far less likely to snipe in the future. Without a camouflage that works, sniping just isn't possible.

Sometimes, however, the Sniper will take the opportunity to tell you just what it is that you're doing wrong. This is your cue to assess critically the Sniper's claims.

Seek Group Confirmation or Denial of the Sniper's Criticism.

After you have stood up to the Sniper, be ready to discuss the underlying problem, but not before you're sure that you're not just, even more subtly, being harpooned. Remember that the basic motivation of hostile people is to prove to themselves and others around them that their ideas about how things should be done are *right*. Their first impulse, therefore, is to tell you what to do or to complain disgustedly about what you're doing. It is important that you *don't* capitulate to these criticisms, even if they touch on actions of yours about which you feel guilty or insecure.

If the Sniper has said, "This is the worst-planned meeting I've ever had to suffer through," don't reply, "Well, what can we do to improve it?" Although on the surface this is a reasonable and nondefensive response, it carries the implicit assumption that the accusation is completely true—just the affirmation that the Sniper wants. Problem-solving on this basis would end with you feeling dissatisfied and resentful, and with the Sniper's view of the world apparently validated.

A better reply would be: "Anyone else see it that way?" Whatever the response from the group, you will have broadened the measure of reality to include the opinions of everyone. Then, if the Sniper's criticism is supported, you can immediately try to ferret out the problem. If the others don't agree that your meeting is the world's worst, follow up with: "I guess there is a difference of opinion" (not: "See, you're wrong"), then: "Can you be more specific?"

In general, your response should neither directly contradict the Sniper's allegations nor allow them to pass as objective truth.

Deal with the Problems.

When you feel ready, move on to consider whatever problems may be underlying the sniping. Remember that Snipers will be quick to tell you what to do. Their remedies may or may not be sound. If they seem unfeasible or incomplete, be careful not to dismiss the problem along with the unworkable solutions. Instead, probe behind the solutions to the specifics of the problem that they are intended to solve. There are excellent reference materials available that suggest techniques for analyzing and solving problems in an active and vigorous way. You'll find several in the reference list at the end of this book.

PREVENTION

Sniping behavior can to some extent be prevented by providing a special time and place for those concerned to bring up problems and issues for discussion. For example, regular work-team meetings give subordinates or associates an opportunity and a serious invitation to raise topics that are bothering them. Even though it would seem that staff members could, and ought to, bring up problems in the absence of specially constructed meetings, they usually don't. When it's been called to their attention, most supervisors, like most parents, recognize that most of their day-to-day communications focus on specific and short-run problems. The longer-range concerns and general irritants or inefficiencies tend to be passed over until they elicit the difficult behaviors we have been discussing in this book.

An additional benefit of providing a regular forum for airing grievances is that *you* will know that you have provided an opportunity for issues to be raised and dealt with constructively. Under fire, the knowledge that you have done your part should help you to remain firm when bringing the hostility of the Sniper to the surface.

THIRD PARTY INTERVENTIONS

Being a witness to the sniping of someone else is an uncomfortable, even painful experience. While the temptation might be to intervene under these circumstances, I suggest you consider the situation carefully before deciding to proceed.

Proceed at Your Own Risk.

There are three main reasons why it may be wise to avoid intervening as a third party in a sniping attack.

First, some people choose to live with the abrasive behavior of others. They may tolerate sniping because they fear something worse; they may value other qualities of the Sniper so greatly that they're content to put up with an occasional pot shot; they may get a perverse sense of enjoyment from it. Whether or not it is in their best interests to make this choice, the right to allow oneself to be hurt by another cannot practically be denied.

Second, to intervene as a peacemaker in a conflict, there must exist at least three elements: the desire on both sides to resolve the conflict; a commitment to continue talking until a mutually agreed upon stopping point has been reached; and a mutual respect for the neutrality of the third party. None of these circumstances is likely to pertain to the observer of Sniper attacks. Remember, too, that the common fate of peacemakers is often to be scorned by both parties.

Finally, you should recognize that it is those who are being sniped at who are in the *best* position to cope, because they are chief characters in the interaction.

Intervene on Your Own Behalf.

None of this suggests that you should have to sit through a sniping session when you *do* find it upsetting. In that circumstance, you are properly intervening for yourself, not for the victim. The coping method in this instance is simple. You must make known your observation that hostility is being expressed by the Sniper. It is doing so in a matter-of-fact way, without elaboration or involvement in the fight that is the key. But the sniping financial analyst in our example at the beginning of this section was stopped by another analyst who responded to one of Burt's smiling cuts at Stan with "Why don't you and he fight?" It was said with a wry smile, and an immediate return to conversation with someone else. As you might guess, this did not stop Burt's sniping. However, he *did* stop sniping at Stan whenever that particular analyst was around.

REVIEW OF COPING WITH SNIPERS

—Smoke them out. Don't let social convention stop you.
—Provide the Sniper with an alternative to a direct contest.
—Don't capitulate to the Sniper's view of the situation. Get other points of view.
—Do move on to try to solve any problems that are uncovered.
—Prevent sniping by setting up regular problem-solving meetings.
—If you are a third party to the sniping, stay out of the middle but do insist that it stop in front of you.

THE EXPLODER

The behavioral peculiarity of the Exploder, the third type of Hostile-Aggressive person we are examining in this chapter, is what I call the adult tantrum, because it looks and sounds so much like the frustrated, hurting rage that I have seen in children. In adults, tantrums are fearsome attacks filled with rage that seems barely under control. Resistance or provocation, intended or not, can cause an escalation of fury to the point where paper-weights are thrown, blows are struck, or unforgivable and unforgettable things are said. It is particularly unnerving that such behavior often erupts during a discussion that appeared at the start to be friendly and reasonable. It is this quality that makes the label Exploder seem apt.

RECOGNIZING AND UNDERSTANDING THE BEHAVIOR

An adult tantrum is a sudden, almost automatic response to a situation in which a person feels both thwarted and psychologically threatened. In the absence of frustration, the situation may elicit only some internal feelings of distrust and suspicion. Without the threat, the blockage alone might be handled with whatever positive psychological strengths and strategies that person has developed. It is the combination that is volatile. The words or actions that represent a threat may be subtle, unintended, or only partially intended. Frequently, the very fact that something is seen as threatening is outside the awareness of both parties. When sparked in some way, the Exploder feels first angry and then blaming or suspicious. Meanwhile, the object of the tantrum, being quite unaware of having said anything wrong, is likely to feel surprised and bewildered at the abrupt and horrifying change in the situation.

A CASE EXAMPLE

Terry's case provides a good illustration of the behavior that characterizes an Exploder, and the sequence of threat and resistance that evokes it. You might want to see if you can catch the offensive words that set Terry off.

Terry is the thirtyish head manager of a dynamic advertising agency. He is known to his staff as a brilliant problem solver, a hard worker with high expectations, and a person of considerable charm and political sense. He has also shown a genuine sensitivity to the personal needs of his staff.

Yet Terry has also sown the seeds of distrust, timidity, and indecisiveness in his entire staff, and several of his most able people have taken salary cuts just to get away from him. It's not difficult to see why.

At a recent staff meeting, to take just one instance, Terry, his account executives, and several specialists in marketing and media coverage are reviewing a memo that Terry had written after returning from a trade convention. The memo describes in detail a new marketing approach recently taken by a chief competitor.

TERRY: I believe that we need to make an aggressive response. Everyone should come up with ideas for our own campaign, buttonhole local trade association people, generally call in all the chips we've got out, and move.

RUSSELL (an account executive): Well, sometimes you can make something big out of a minor league effort. Wouldn't we be better off holding fire for a while?

TERRY: Oh, you think so?

TIM (another account executive): Yeah, I remember three years ago when they tried a saturation campaign, and it just ran out of gas. Let's just not get all excited . . .

TERRY (interrupting in a voice that becomes increasingly shrill): What's wrong with you people? You would never do anything if I didn't push you. I suppose everyone here wants to sit back with his head up his butt and wait until it's too late. I'm the only one who really cares about this office. Get the hell out of here.

Terry was yelling by his time, punctuating each word with a stamp of his foot on the floor. The rest of the group sit, eyes fixed on the table top, afraid, ashamed, angry at Terry, themselves, and each other.

It was at another meeting of this group, suggested by me as a way of analyzing why they were having planning problems, that this particular incident was untangled. Russell was able to clarify what he had said: "Sometimes you can make something big out of a minor league effort." The "you" he was referring to was not Terry, but *anyone*. Terry, however, always sensitive to criticism of his competence, had interpreted it as ridicule of him and as an attempt to shoot down his plan for a marketing counterattack. When Tim supported Russell ("Let's just not get all excited"), Terry felt completely unappreciated. For some people, none of this would have been felt as personally threatening, but for Terry it clearly was.

Exploders appear more out of control of themselves than Snipers or Sherman Tanks. To those who have them, tantrums happen, they are not planned. It is this lack of prior intentionality that distinguishes tantrums from other kinds of hostile behavior. At times, as in Terry's case, there is a hysterical quality to the outburst, expressed through tears or speechless rage. While observers may talk about Sherman Tanks or Snipers as mean, vicious, or terrifying, they more often use such words as "over-emotional," "super-touchy," and "irritable" to describe Exploders.

THE EFFECTS OF ADULT TANTRUMS

Why do Exploders respond to perceived threats by losing control? Adult tantrums are grownup versions of early learned defensive tactics designed to cope with fear, helplessness, and frustration. To a child, tantrums are a great equalizing mechanism. Like a revolver in the hands of a weakling, they give real power to make or reverse important, even critical, decisions (to a child, being able to eat ice cream before dinner can become a critical matter).

In the case of Exploders, such eruptive behavior stays in their repertoire because the outbursts still "work," at least on the surface. They can be quite effective in reducing otherwise well-functioning adults to silence, passivity, or tantrums of their own. Yet tantrum behavior produces a greater backwash of anger and resistance than any of the other difficult behaviors. For this reason, wanting to understand it is just what most people are not motivated to do. This is unfortunate, however, because understanding what makes the Exploder erupt is a necessary first step in coping with the behavior.

COPING WITH EXPLODERS

Coping with a person having a tantrum is chiefly a matter of helping him or her regain self-control. With young children, you do this most effectively by nonpunitive but firm physical control. They need to be physically immobilized by arms around them if they are small enough (or if the controller is big enough), or by wrists held, if they are striking out, or by isolation in "the big yellow chair" or their own room for a time. Within the confines of these firm but benevolent limits, they are free from the interaction that may have touched off the explosion, and they can, at length, compose themselves.

To cope with adults you follow an analogous procedure.

Give Them Time to Run Down.

It is just not possible to cope with an Exploder if you can't be heard. Some people get through the worst and loudest part of their explosion rather quickly. Therefore, it is usually worthwhile to wait for them to run down. Often, suddenly realizing where they are and what they're doing, Exploders will become suddenly silent, or will burst into tears. However, if no pause occurs, then *you* need to try to douse the fire yourself. These are phrases that I have found often work well: "Stop! Stop!" "Wait a minute!" "Right! Right!" or "Yes! Yes!" The repetition helps, as does a sharp inflection or enough volume to break through. Perhaps because it is unexpected, yelling "Right!" or "Yes!" seems to have a singular effect in halting the outburst.

You must get the attention of a person having a tantrum if you're going to break his or her self-imposed spell. Standing up or sitting down may help. Be as dramatic as you need to be. Rising suddenly and shouting the person's name can do wonders in getting everyone's attention.

Show Your Serious Intentions.

Even before you are sure you have the attention of the person in a tantrum state, make it loudly clear that you take him or her seriously. For example, as soon as you've yelled "Stop! Stop!" go right on with: "I can see that this is very important to you and it is to me. I want to discuss it with you, but not this way!" Be ready to repeat these threat-reducing statements several times, *loudly*, before they have an effect.

Interrupt the Interaction.

If the steps we've discussed don't help, or even if they do, try to get a breather. Announce a break in the meeting, even if you're not in charge, or just leave, making sure to say, "I'll be back." Your purposes are to buy time to compose yourself, to break the immediate pattern of interaction between yourself and the Exploder, and to help him or her regain self-control.

One way to achieve this cooling-down effect, and also make the situation less tense for both of you, is to move to a place where you can continue the discussion privately. A head nurse who was the object of a physician's hysterical rantings helped matters immensely by saying, "I want to hear everything you have to say about nursing on this ward, but *not* here where it will disturb everyone. Come into my office." With this said, she turned on her heel, walked into her office and sat down. By the time the doctor had reached her office he had cooled down some, and they were then able to have a useful discussion. He did not, by the way, ever yell at her again.

COPING IN PRACTICE

With the above in mind, let's now revisit the meeting that was disrupted by Terry's emotional outburst. What might it have sounded like if his staff had coped more effectively?

TERRY: I believe that we need to make an aggressive response. Everyone should come up with ideas for our own campaign, buttonhole local trade association people, generally call in all the chips we've got out, and move.

RUSSELL: Well, sometimes you can mage something big out of a minor league effort. Wouldn't we be better off holding fire for a while?

TERRY: Oh, you think so?

TIM: Yeah, I remember three years ago when they tried a saturation campaign, and it just ran out of gas. Let's just not get all excited . . .

TERRY (interrupting in a voice that becomes increasingly shrill): What's wrong with you people? You would never do anything if I didn't push you. I suppose everyone here wants to sit back with his head up his butt and wait until it's too late. I'm the only one who really cares about this office. Get out of here . . .

RUSSELL (interrupting loudly): Wait a minute, Terry! Something's gone wrong! (He stands up.) I think we need to do something about the campaign, and I'm *serious*. (The last said with a slap on the table.) Could we take a break right now and then come back for a planning discussion?

TERRY (as if coming out of a daze): Uh, oh, yeah, that's a good idea. Back in ten minutes.

RUSSELL: Can you and I get together in a few minutes, Terry?

TERRY: Oh, sure.

The turnaround in Terry's behavior may seem sudden and contrived to you. But do all attempts at coping with Exploders work so well? At the risk of straining your credulity, in most of the situations I've witnessed, dramatic changes have occurred when adult tantrums are interrupted the way I have described. Terry's story in fact is true, and one of his staff did learn to intervene when he started to erupt. It helped Terry a great deal to acknowledge that when he exploded he really lost control of himself. Even more important was his admission to Russell during a prior consulting session that *he* did not like what happened to him, and that he wanted to stop. This gave Russell the permission he needed to say, "Wait a minute. Something's gone wrong!"

REVIEW OF COPING WITH EXPLODERS

—Give them time to run down and regain self-control on their own.
—If they don't, break into their tantrum state by saying or shouting a neutral phrase such as "Stop!"
—Show that you take them seriously.
—If needed and possible, get a breather and get some privacy with them.

SOME FURTHER SUGGESTIONS ON COPING WITH HOSTILE-AGGRESSIVE BEHAVIOR

In learning to cope with any type of Hostile-Aggressive person, whether Sherman Tank, Sniper, or Exploder, there are two further suggestions that you might bear in mind: practice on the less extreme forms of difficult behavior first, and be clear that you are in the presence of hostility before applying the coping steps appropriate for dealing with difficult behavior.

Cope with Less Extreme Forms of Difficult Behavior First.

Hostile-Aggressive behavior is not always as extreme as the examples I've used might indicate. Sherman Tanks are at times polite while running over others; Snipers are often so witty that even their targets are not sure whether they've been shepherded or shorn; and the tantrums of an Exploder are sometimes confined to a few tears or a little swearing. This fact needs to be kept in mind, because the coping steps we have looked at in this chapter are easier to try when the behavior is not excessive. You, therefore, have an opportunity to practice the steps in a low-risk situation before taking on the more imposing behaviors. This is always useful, because coping with Hostile-Aggressive people can be *very* difficult and most of us need all the help we can get. More importantly, by coping effectively with less extreme behavior you may actually prevent some of the worst from arising.

Hostility May Be in the Eye of the Beholder.

To people who are not themselves aggressive, even a moderate and productive use of such behavior can seem excessive. If you know yourself to be a person who approaches life nonaggressively, you might do well to find a standard by which to judge your reactions to pushy, attacking, or over-emotional people. Observe the responses of others in the same or similar situations. Ask yourself these questions when you begin to feel irritated or offended by a seemingly hostile person:

—Is *this* aggressive behavior appropriate to the situation, even though *I* might never act that way? For example, it is appropriate to tell surly salespeople that their demeanor is offensive and unacceptable.
—Am I seeing a useful venting of relevant pent-up feelings, or is this a bona fide tantrum?
—Am I hearing active and unvarnished disagreement, the purpose of which is to get at the facts, as a hostile or derogatory attack?

It is important to make these distinctions, because treating aggressiveness as if it were hostility may incite just the behavior you find difficult. When aggressive people run into obstacles, they tend to deal with them directly and forcefully. If they sense resentment, or worse, unresponsiveness, when they're just trying to get at the facts, even ordinarily nonhostile aggressives can become provoked to anger.

Chapter 3

"AND ANOTHER THING . . ."—THE COMPLEAT COMPLAINER

Imagine yourself a supervisor in an office responsible for processing a large amount of paperwork. A fellow supervisor approaches your desk, sits down (Complainers usually sit down because they know they're going to be staying for a while), and starts off with this:

Why is the work that is supposed to come from your section to mine always late? You know it's supposed to get to our office by 9:45 A.M., but it's been getting later and later. And it really holds us up when we have to wait for you—and you know I tried to call you yesterday but the line is always busy, and when it wasn't busy nobody ever answered it. And I've sent you a lot of memos about this and I never get any answer from you. I never had this trouble with any other supervisor, and I don't know why we're having this trouble now [eyes traveling around the room] . . . You know, I don't really like the way the rooms are painted here, and I think the rug really doesn't match anything else, and . . .

THE BEHAVIOR

Can you hear the music that accompanies those words? Sentences, connected with ands and buts, that flow without pause. A whining, almost singsong quality that self-righteously blames and accuses. These are the telltale signs of the Complainer. Complainers may not be the

most Difficult People to get on with. They do not cause
consternation and fear as do Hostile-Aggressives, nor are
they as overbearing and pompous as Know-It-All Experts, whom we'll meet in Chapter 7. Yet, as that arch-
complainer Jonah discovered, even God at times finds
them irksome, irritating, and very exhausting.

Complainers are those Difficult People who manage to
find fault with everything, malcontents who gripe ad
nauseam about everything from how messy your desk is
to the temperature outside. The disguised message behind
all these gripes is that "someone," usually meaning you,
should be doing something about them. Complainers are
the people you find yourself automatically placating or
becoming defensive with, whether or not you've done anything wrong.

Complainers, as we are using the label here, should
not be confused with people who have a legitimate complaint and are simply trying to bring it to someone's attention, or with those individuals who just need to get
something off their chests. While those folks who merely
have problems and are quite properly focusing attention
on them to get something done surely have complaints,
they differ sharply from Complainers in the way they
present them, and in what they hope to get from the
situation. Problem solvers, unlike genuine Complainers,
are primarily interested in finding solutions to concrete
problems, even though initially they let you know about
the problem in a way that makes their anger and exasperation clear.

What can be even more perplexing about sorting out
Complainers from those with legitimate problems is that
there is usually some substance to Complainers' accusations. The truth may be that your section's work *has*
fallen behind, your staff *does* let the phone ring too
long, you *are* a new and unfinished supervisor who has
replaced a competent older hand. It is this knack for
stating problems as convincing accusations that gives such
power to complaining. After all, if you become skilled at
truculantly blaming others when something goes wrong,
those others can be kept occupied with the necessity of
being defensive. Certainly they will be too busy to hold
the Complainer accountable for meeting their, or anyone
else's, expectations.

Skilled Complainers have the accusatory style down so

well that they can easily turn the tables on their bosses, putting them immediately on the defensive. For example, Rosemary, head of a small ticket office, described what happened when she queried Helen, one of her agents, about an accounting difficulty:

ROSEMARY: We've found some more errors in the cash reconcilement, Helen. Are you sure . . .

HELEN: If you'd only realize that I'm always careful, you wouldn't keep bringing it to me. There's no written procedure for handling money, and you know it. I've told you before but you still haven't gotten the accountant to write one.

ROSEMARY: I know we need a better procedure, but . . .

HELEN: We don't even have *any* procedure. It's not my job to do anything but take ticket orders and put everything where I'm told, and besides . . .

Complainers also differ markedly from those emotionally overloaded people who occasionally need to let feelings spill out. Some individuals feel things more vividly than others. To keep their own tension levels under control, they need a person with whom their feelings can be put into words and thus made more manageable. Even those of us whose threshold of emotional reaction is higher can sometimes use opportunities to think out loud about conflicts with the boss, frustrations over a failed project, or humiliations in front of co-workers, in order to make the feelings more understandable and thus more bearable. Simply venting, however, is not the same as secretly accusing the listener of causing our woes; we merely want a sympathetic ear to help us handle some temporary emotional storms.

The Triangular Complainer.

There's one species of Complainer who differs in an important respect from standard, dump-directly-on-you Complainers. Triangular Complainers don't complain *at* you, they complain *to* you about other terrible people. Frequent targets are managers or supervisors, parents of siblings, and professional caretakers, but anyone may be selected as a potential depository for a Triangular Complainer's rotten eggs. Here is Paula's description of the experience:

I am *so* tired of hearing from one of my typists about everything that's wrong in the office. Yesterday she stayed late to tell me about Roger. He doesn't answer his phone before 9:00 A.M.; he's behind on his stat reports; he's been shopping at the discount store during working hours; and so on and so on. The worst part of it all is that I suspect that Marilee is probably right about Roger. So I don't just tell her to stop. It sounds terrible to say it, but I'm afraid I'll miss something about him that I ought to know. But I feel sneaky and I find myself explaining away all of her points. "You haven't tried calling him every day, have you?" I say to Marilee, as if it were all a joke. I end up just feeling *tired*. To top it all, while I keep on thinking and worrying about what she says about Roger, I don't really do anything about it.

Most people feel somewhat uneasy as a party to such tattling. Even more frustrating is a vague awareness that the tattled information cannot readily be used in a way that does not, in itself, contain subterfuge. What can Paula do with Marilee's information? She can play detective, making accusations, citing vague, hearsay evidence, or she can try to pretend she hasn't heard anything. In the face of this ambiguity, it's no wonder that most people, like Paula, end up just feeling tired. In any case, victims of Triangular Complainers, like targets of their more straightforward cousins, are likely to find themselves caught in a web of rambling accusations that leaves them frustrated and unproductive.

UNDERSTANDING COMPLAINERS

To cope successfully with Complainers you need to know what lies behind their actions and how easy it is to be sucked into their accusatory world. Consider this example. The Complainer is Jerry, neatly dressed, a little overweight and father of one of the new members of a Boy Scout troop. Jerry has cornered Mary, an active volunteer involved in the leadership of the troop, over coffee after a meeting.

JERRY: You know, Mac [the Scoutmaster] is awfully hard on the boys. He just keeps pushing them too hard. Boys need a chance to do things on their own, and I don't really think that it's so important that all the detailed merit badge requirements be satisfied, don't you agree?

MARY (hesitantly): Well, I suppose . . .

JERRY: I've talked to a bunch of other people in the troop and they all agree, and they think that something ought to be done about it.

MARY: Well, I think that Mac is trying to do his best . . .

JERRY (interrupting): He really should be making scouting fun for the boys, not work, and I don't think that he's really doing that and something really ought to be done soon, but it probably won't be, and . . .

Even Jerry's seeming rationality does not shut out the accusing, prescriptive, yet defeated quality typical of Complainers. Needless to say, Complainers don't feel that they are whining. From the inside, complaining is an effort, albeit foredoomed, to warn about a thing gone wrong that *someone else* must fix. When the whining quality is pointed out to a Complainer, it is most often met with a lack of comprehension about what is meant and an insistence that the problems are real and not imagined. "In the face of seeming doubt, reaffirm the truth of your allegations" is the maxim that fuels the large quantity of verbiage that Complainers such as Jerry manufacture.

Three factors in the Complainers' view of the world combine to convert useful problem solving into complaining: they find themselves powerless, prescriptive, and perfect.

Powerless. Human beings vary in the degree to which they believe that they have control over what happens to them. Most of us, of course, believe that what we encounter in life results from mixtures of luck, our own brilliance or stupidity, and the good or bad things that others do to us or for us. A few are sure that they are sole makers of their own fates—we'll meet one of them later when we discuss those Know-It-All Experts, the Bulldozers. Complainers, however, fall into that group that feels powerless in the management of their own lives, as if the causes of all that happens to them lie outside their grasp. From this passive view, all that goes well can be attributed to good luck or to favors from benevolent others. Effort, ingenuity, and ability are, in this light, without significant power to affect anything.

Similarly, roadblocks and frustrations can only be removed by getting others, the truly powerful ones, first to pay heed, and then to take action.

The persistence of this sense of being without practical power to change things in the face of opposing forces comes through in this observation by a small company's production manager about one of his lead-men.

> Have you talked to Herman yet? Oh, he knows his work well enough, but he's always griping. He seems to believe that the only reason that new equipment items aren't approved is because the boss doesn't understand our problems. I have tried to point out other possibilities—bum economic conditions or that he hasn't really put down all the facts. But all I get from him is a lot of badmouthing about how no one really cares. He'll probably complain to you that I won't promote him because I don't understand all that he does around here. Even there, he thinks that whether or not he gets promoted depends completely on whether or not *I* want it.

Prescriptive. If fatalism were the only underlying factor, contented, resigned acceptance, not complaining, would result. You would float down the river of life, accepting the good, putting up with the bad, secure in the belief that personal attributes or efforts count for nothing. To feel put upon, one must have an image of the way things *ought* to be and a galling sense of injustice that they are not that way. This prescriptive quality permeates almost everything that Complainers say. A complaint that your work is late implies that it should be on time. In Jerry's complaints to Mary he clearly has strong ideas about the way Mac should behave as a Scoutmaster. That Mac doesn't fit that mold, however, brings forth not some direct action, but rather a petulant wish that "someone" would get Mac to behave as he is supposed to.

Perfect. Complainers persist in their ritual behavior because complaining keeps them appearing blameless, innocent, and morally perfect, at least to themselves. Complainers gain self-validation as "good" people twice: first, by placing the responsibility for the ills they observe on others, and, second, having done that, in the comparison of their relative "goodness" to others' demonstrated "badness." The Complainer thinks: "I've brought this to your attention, told you that it's not the way it should be. I've done all I can. Now it's up to you." Having established that it's you, not they, who are at fault, and that nothing yet has been done to right those wrongs they've pointed out, they become even more righteously angry at you for not doing what you should, and could, do.

Because of their prescriptive way of thinking, it's especially important for Complainers to validate their belief that they are without responsibility. To believe otherwise would force them to see themselves as mere carping hypocrites rather than as noble, if powerless, fighters for the right.

While the act of complaining itself may hold a comfort for the Complainer that is not related to the issues themselves, it is also usually a successful short-term strategy for catching our attention. Complainers are hard to ignore. They tempt our desire for secret information. Their sense of powerlessness creates a vacuum that sucks in some people who have a strong wish to help others. At times they even provide a convenient vehicle for the expression of vague work- or family-related tensions as they pick at the "sores" of poor organizational functioning that have not been acknowledged, much less cured, by bosses. While others in the group may not feel nearly as powerless or pessimistic, they may nonetheless get caught up in the litany of complaints against those in authority. Triangular Complainers further provide the added attraction of leaving most of us feeling superior. We feel superior both to the Complainer for being ineffectual and to the subject of the complaint for having sinned. Thus, we get two satisfactions for the price of one, an "entertainment" hard to turn down.

While Complainers do get attention, they seldom get action. Impatience, patronizing dismissal, oversolicitous personal attention, or simply avoidance are more often their lot. We can't help, for instance, but sympathize with the salesman who told me:

> I have been avoiding a customer that I should be cultivating. He is a steady purchaser of one of our slower-moving lines. It's curious that it worries me, but I haven't been back in a month. As soon as I come through the door this guy hits me with how long it's been since I've come around and how hard it is to

reach me by phone. Then he starts in on the line: too many changes in style, poor workmanship—you name it, we do it wrong. I reached the point where servicing him was throwing off my whole day.

Faced with avoidance or placating responses, the Complainer, after a time, accurately perceives that nothing is being done. Thus the sad linkage is once more closed; the Complainer is further confirmed as a powerless victim of unjust forces, and thus leads not to constructive action but to even more self-righteous complaining. For the Triangular Complainer the situation is equally self-defeating, because the subject of the complaints remains in the dark and thus cannot solve the problem, even if he or she wanted to. Scoutmaster Mac, for instance, never did get feedback that might have been useful to him. The troop continued to lose boys who were offended by the overscolding and who didn't hang around long enough to appreciate Mac's genuine leadership ability. And Jerry became even more dissatisfied.

COMPLAINERS IN REVIEW

—Complainers point out real problems, but they do it in a manner that elicits placating or defensive responses from others. Their frustration at the lack of constructive problem solving is genuine, but self-defeating, since it leads to more complaining.
—Complaining can be understood as the only kind of active behavior that seems possible to those who feel powerless to determine their own fate. That is, they believe that the causes of what happens to them are attributable to benevolent or malevolent others.
—Complainers have a strong sense of how others ought to behave; they feel genuine, if sometimes disguised, anger when those others do not conform.
—Complaining is self-validating since it provides a solid basis for Complainers to confirm their own lack of responsibility for anything that is not done well. They can continue to feel personally "perfect."

COPING WITH COMPLAINERS

The key to successfully coping with Complainers is to break their self-confirming cycle of passivity, blaming others, and powerlessness, and to insist that a problem-solving perspective be taken toward their complaints. Here's how to do this.

Listen Attentively.

Look in on Doreas, who is having her weekly management meeting with Fred, her boss. This meeting is moving through a familiar, if tiresome, sequence: Doreas begins with a long litany against Mrs. Rogers, the division head. Then she moves on to tear down her two favorite subordinates (they must be favorites because she spends so much time chronicling exactly what they're doing wrong), and finally she hints that Fred has been away too much recently. After six months of these meetings, Fred no longer bothers to listen. He sits, impassively at first, then the small signs of impatience creep in. He glances at his watch. He fashions paper clips into triangles and diamonds. Under the desk, his foot begins to swing back and forth. At length, he stands, mutters something about an appointment, and drops a rapid "See you" as he heads for the door.

Fred's wish to escape is very understandable. Listening with serious attention to a Complainer can be an extraordinarily demanding task. I confess that I have always found it confoundedly difficult to listen well to Complainers. My inner voice keeps saying, "For God's sake, stop whining."

Unfortunately, even though it is not easy, listening attentively to Complainers is a necessary first step in coping with them. Listening is a powerful interpersonal tool for connecting solidly with anyone, difficult or not, if it is the right kind of listening done at the appropriate time, done with skill, and, most importantly, done attentively. It is particularly important with Complainers for four specific reasons. First, it provides an opportunity for the Complainer simply to let off steam. Putting problems into words provides a release for frustration, fear, anger over assumed slights—any of the myriad feelings that can underlie something that's gone wrong. Recall that Complainers feel passive anger. Without an opportunity to relieve this pressure they cannot move to more constructive problem solving. Second, being heard can lessen that sense of being "dismissed" and powerlessness that will trigger an even greater outpouring of complaints. Third, listening provides information that you'll need in order to carry out the next coping step. Finally, by listening attentively you may discover that the person who is complaining to you is merely looking for a sympathetic ear and is not a Complainer at all.

Acknowledge.

The second coping step is to acknowledge what the Complainer has said. You acknowledge others when you actively let them know that you *have* understood what they've said to you, that you know how they feel, and that you take them seriously. The simplest way to do this is to paraphrase what you think their main points have been, ending with your best guess about how the Complainer must feel about the terrible situation being described. Here's what your acknowledgment might have sounded like to that office supervisor who complained that your work was always late:

> Wait a minute, wait a minute, let's see if I understand what you've been saying to me. Okay, since last Friday, it seems to you that the work from our section hasn't been arriving in your office until 10:30. Your need is to have it by 9:45 so that it doesn't interrupt your own work flow. You remember calling twice last week and it seemed to you that the phone rang eight or nine times before it was answered. You wrote me a memo about this, but you are pretty sure it was two weeks before I replied. Right now you're feeling pretty frustrated about the whole thing.

Be Prepared to Interrupt

To acknowledge, you may have to interrupt. The flow of verbiage from some Complainers seems endless; a series of statements strung together by *and*'s and *but*'s may offer few openings for you to jump in gracefully. But once you've discovered the gist of their complaints, stop them, as politely as you can, but firmly. By taking control of the structure of the conversation—for example, who speaks when about what—you immediately lessen the "value" of complaints to the Complainer.

Use Limiting Responses.

Complainers love words like *always* and *never*. They will allege that you *never* make phone calls or that the work is *always* late. You help them to gain more of a problem-solving perspective, the eventual goal of these coping steps, when your acknowledgments are made in a way that pins down the complaints to specific times, places, or facts. This should only be done, however, when you have accurate information. Trying to persuade by subtly changing the facts will only produce distrust and probably more complaining. If you *do* remember when the unanswered phone calls were made, however, it helps to say so. Your acknowledgment then becomes: "You called on Tuesday and Friday, and at those times, at any rate, it took eight or nine rings before the phone was answered."

Don't Agree.

If acknowledgment is useful, agreement is not. Acknowledgment conveys understanding and elicits a sense of being genuinely noticed. Agreement, on the other hand, confirms to the Complainer that you are indeed responsible for the existence of the problems. The difference is crucial. Here, for example, is the acknowledging statement, previously given, changed to an agreeing statement.

> You're telling me that the work from our section has been late and that you've had trouble getting in touch with me. Well, you're right. We've been running behind for the last month, and I've been trying to get my people to answer the phone quicker. I'm really sorry that you've had trouble.

On the face of it, this simple statement merely owns up to some slippage on your part that has caused the Complainer inconvenience. It is both a candid acceptance of responsibility and a statement of regret, both honorable and completely proper things to do. Except when you are dealing with Complainers. It's not that they don't respond actively to confessions, especially when they are accompanied by an apology. It's that they respond in a way that interferes with any practical resolution of the problem.

To understand why apologizing, or even a simple agreement, doesn't do the job with Complainers, consider first your own reaction the next time someone—other than a member of your family—trips over your feet. The "ouch" will likely be met with an "Oh, I'm sorry." That apology will not be simply a statement of regret about a troublesome event. It will be part of a learned social sequence: an indirect plea for forgiveness to which you're expected to reply, "Oh, that's all right." This sequence probably developed as a useful social mechanism for avoiding fights, but there is a negative side to it.

Think of yourself the second after a guest in your house has, while clowning around, dropped your favorite family heirloom, a fragile porcelain bowl. Although you may squeeze out a "Don't worry about it," of course it *isn't* really all right! You feel the loss. You feel angry at your guest for being careless. Yet you have been "forced" to say the opposite. By this strange twist, the person who caused the trouble becomes the injured party. You who suffered the loss are doing the consoling.

The opportunity that this learned sequence gives to a wrongdoer is surely hard to resist. A timely "Gee, I goofed" has turned a potential scolding into a comforting for many a child. Consequently, the admission of guilt as a social maneuver is easily evoked from some of us. The negative side, of course, is that, while it dissipates the hassle of the moment, it does not lead to productive problem solving. An admission of guilt fixes blame without regard for the complexities that underlie *any* problem. While your guest may have been clowning around when the bowl was dropped, for instance, what was an heirloom doing on the table at a party anyway? And, after all, you were the one who invited the clown in the first place.

With Complainers, admitting wrongdoing, even in the short run—to get out from under a verbal barrage, perhaps—probably won't work. To the contrary, if you wish to make sure that you get more than your fair share of complaining, admit that they are right and that you are at fault. Expect the dialogue to go something like this:

"Well, we *have* been getting behind in our work. I'm really sorry that it's caused you so much trouble."

"And you ought to be sorry. Now let me tell you about all the other things you're doing wrong."

Your admission to Complainers that you are at fault is not only likely to be taken as a sign of submission, but, more importantly, you are just confirming their belief that the power to solve the problems that they are pointing out is, in truth, yours. You validate for them the fact that indeed it's all your fault and they are blameless.

Avoid the Accusation-Defense-Reaccusation Sequence.

After acknowledging, but not agreeing with, the Complainer's gripes, it is important to move as quickly as you can into problem solving. The principal reason for this is to avoid becoming caught up in an insidious communication sequence that Complainers love. It has been most accurately called the accusation-defense-reaccusation pattern and was first identified in troubled families. In the old-fashioned nuclear family setting, the A-D-R pattern surfaces something like this:

HE (with a tone of helpless frustration): I don't have any clean shirts to wear [Heard as an *accusation*.]

SHE: Well, you know, the children haven't been feeling well the last few days and I was so busy with them yesterday, and besides, the washing machine hasn't been working very well, and I had another one of my headaches . . . [*Defense*.]

SHE (with rising anger): . . . and if you'd only put your dirty shirts into the hamper right away, and besides that, if you made more money and bought more shirts, then we wouldn't have this problem. [*Reaccusation*.]

The initial statement may or may not have been intended as an accusation. Heard as an accusation, it received a "rational" defense, and was followed by an escalating reaccusation. The reaccusation can, in turn, be counted on to receive another defense and that defense a reattack, continued, at times, to a painful and deep impasse. At that point *any* statement by either of the parties may be heard as an accusation: "Nice day we're having." "Now what do you mean by that? I don't have anything to do with the weather . . ."

Few of us have escaped involvement in this fascinating process. Although it shows most clearly in the family, I have found it as common in work, school, and community settings. To be sure, there it is often veneered with politeness and indirection and is thus more difficult to detect and to deal with. As Don Jackson, an early researcher in the family as a communication system, has pointed out, the most insidious aspect is that A-D-R can sound on the surface like a useful discussion of a problem. In reality, of course, it interferes with problem solving.

It is important to understand the A-D-R sequence because, in coping with Complainers, those skillful master-accusers, it is an odds-on favorite that your own defensive reactions will be hooked. After all, haven't most of us been brought up to feel slightly defensive when anything goes wrong? As it was passed on to our parents, and from them to us, we continue to pass on to our children a belief that there is always a culprit. If the milk spills, Gregory must have been careless; if Rick gets a "D" in math, he must not have studied enough. The degree to which this unplanned teaching permeates the child's world is captured by that story of the mother whose little boy was upstairs during an earthquake. In response to her frantic cry of "Johnny, Johnny!" he answered, "I didn't do it, Mother, I didn't do it."

A-D-R confirms to both parties that the focus of blame is, and ought to be, on the other person. Although this may be, at end, a self-defeating view, it is certainly a secure one. Therefore, and a very large "therefore" it is, Complainers will, knowingly or unknowingly, keep the pattern alive. That they, as well as their complainees, are annoyed, disgusted, or frustrated just exemplifies Freud's dictum about the behavior of troubled human beings: "They make worse what they seek to cure."

State Facts Without Comment and Apology.

The danger of falling into the A-D-R pattern makes it doubly important for you to acknowledge and state the facts of the case but to do so without apology or editorial comment. Questions of fact often arise during any discussion. With someone who uses complaining strategies, it is particularly important to be as descriptive as possible about them while drawing few, if any, inferences about what the facts might mean. When a Complainer alleges that a letter was sent to you "but it took forever to get an answer," immediately interrupt the conversation. Get the appropriate folder and find the letter in question, with the copy of your reply, if any. Matter-of-factly say, "Well, let's see, yes, here is your letter dated 12 January, and here's the copy of our reply dated 2 February." Put the correspondence back in the folder and say nothing more. No editorial comment, excuse, or explanation, regardless of the length of time between the date of the original letter and of the reply. If, indeed, two months had elapsed between the two pieces of correspondence, let the fact stand by itself. If, instead, it turns out that the reply was sent only six days after the letter was received—not bad for most organizations—it is agonizingly tempting to say, "See! See!" (a defense *and* a reaccusation rolled into one, and this delivered with great economy). Unfortunately, the feeling of sweet satisfaction lasts only until the reply, "Well, I don't care if you have a copy, I never got it until two months later. If your mailing service is as bad as . . ."

Switch to Problem Solving.

The next stage in coping with Complainers is to direct the discussion toward solving the problems the Complainer has raised. Problem solving focuses on what's to be done to make things better in the future. Complaining, on the other hand, reminisces about the history of a problem and assigns blame.

Paradoxically, because of its future orientation, the problem-solving mode can be seen as a way of *avoiding* serious communication about a problem. This is especially true when those involved have strong commitments to or expectations of each other—friends, family members, or business partners, for example. It is tempting at times to sidestep hurts and move too soon past feeling-laden issues to a rational, future-oriented stance. "Let's not go into old history again" may leave no room for some necessary, if painful, reopening of old, still-festering wounds or for working on a clearer expression of complex feelings. Unfortunately, when a reservoir of unacknowledged or unexplored feelings does exist, it can keep a "discussion" moving back and forth over the same old rubble of complaints and cross-complaints. For this reason, problem solving in a family, friendship, or partnership setting needs to be preceded by a particularly thorough effort of acknowledging or airing background issues and feelings.

Pose specific problem-solving questions. With the exception just noted, move into problem solving as soon after the initial coping steps as you can. Actively listen, then acknowledge, then pause slightly (if you pause too long, the Complainer will come in and take over the conversation again). Now pose concrete, descriptive questions that characterize the future-oriented problem-solving mode. For example: "When does the problem occur?" "Are there times when it doesn't occur?" "At what time is it worse or better?" "Who are the particular people most involved?" "What specific things tell you when it's getting worse?" I suggest that you avoid the word *why* even where it might appear appropriate because it often seems to echo parental accusations: "Why did you spill the milk?" "Why did you tease your sister?" *Why* questions serve as invitations to long, defensive justifications or reaccusations rather than matter-of-fact information gathering.

Expect some frustration. If you are dealing with a hard-playing Complainer, don't expect this rational, reality-based approach to work on the first or second try. Your problem-solving attempts may receive no acknowledgment at all or even be followed by a new round of complaining. Expect to be irritated, and to have trouble listening attentively. Heave an inward sigh, interrupt if you have to, paraphrase the complaints, and then move in, once again, with those same problem-solving questions. "Could we get back to the questions I was asking before . . ." will often do it.

Assign limited tasks. When possible, ask the Complainer to collect information relevant to the problem. As a grocery store manager, for example, you might say: "Look, Mrs. Marshall, we're trying to cut down on people having to wait in line so long. Would you keep track for the next two weeks of just how long it takes you to get up to the check-out stand? Just jot down the dates, the times, and how long you've waited."

Or a manager might say to the Complainer in the office: "Look, it would help me to get our section back on the road if you would keep track in the coming two weeks of exactly when the first pieces of work from our section gets to yours."

This is a useful device because it bridges the gap between Complainers' genuine concern and their underlying sense of futility. You provide the drive and the focus to enable them to make the first move. They, however, do all the work. An altogether neat solution.

Get it in writing. Many people gain a sense of greater control over a problem when they have described it in words, and written the words down. I believe that to be the reason that many people have discovered it helpful to ask Complainers to put their complaints in writing.

The cynics among you may now be chuckling over the fact that putting complaints into writing is a lot of work. That's why most people think about writing letters to the editor but never do it. "Write it down!" tests the Complainer's motivation or at least how high on his or her priority list the problems are. However, you can't cope with Complainers simply by indirectly blunting their attacks. That is just what they expect will happen, and they know the proper response—more complaining. Furthermore, if you never get it in writing, issues and problems that ought to be examined may be overlooked. These actions on your part will increase the likelihood that asking for the complaints in writing will actually help: (1) Set a time by which you expect a response. "Could you get a brief outline to me of what you think is wrong by the end of the week? Be as specific about it as you can, Hank." (2) Follow up on your request. "It's Friday and I was expecting your note on those problems, Hank. Can you get it to me by Monday?"

Remember that Complainers are usually on to something, even if they nullify the value of their warnings by the manner in which they are delivered. Supporting *anything* constructive that they do about it will be worth the effort.

The Move of Last Resort.

Ah, but what if none of this works? The Complainer continues to complain at you, the attempt at problem solving doesn't get off the ground, and everything else you do is brushed aside. There is yet a ploy that may turn the tide: Try commenting on the nature of this strange interaction between you and the Complainer.

Once again, interrupt the Complainer and say something like, "Wait a minute, Bill—just how would you like this discussion to end? It's now 2:30. At 2:45 I've got someone else coming in. Where would you like us to be when we're through?"

Of necessity, this must be said without accusing the Complainer of complaining—for me, never easy. I remember many times feeling such fatigued, dull annoyance after a long bout of griping that I was ready to blast my Complainer. Satisfying, but not very useful.

If you are lucky and the circumstances are right, you may get "What? What? Well, uh, I guess what I want is that you'll fix my toaster," or "Well, if your work would just get to our section by 9:45—no later than 10:00 . . ." Of course, this is your cue to move in once again with the problem-solving approach. This time, however, you have had an invitation from the Complainer to do so.

You should expect that the first time you try this ploy it will not work. Complainers, after all, are not very attentive. Their attention is focused on their complaints. Be ready to get back in and try again.

Here's what you might hope for from these efforts: (1) The Complainer will lack self-confirming reinforcement from you, that is, you don't do what you are "supposed" to do—defend, reaccuse, apologize, explain it all away, or walk out—and he or she may stop complaining as much. (2) In the face of your consistent attempts to draw out the practical thinker that is somewhere within, the Complainer may find himself or herself dealing with the situation in a problem-solving way. (3) You may learn about problems you didn't know you had in time to do something about them, with or without the Complainer. (4) Even if this doesn't happen, the Complainer should do the next best thing—go away and find someone more satisfying to complain to. Once again, remember that here we are concerned with coping, not changing or developing.

TRIANGULATING TRIANGLE COMPLAINERS

In addition to these general methods of coping with Complainers, here is a three-point approach for coping with the Triangle Complainers, those Difficult People who tell you incessantly about someone else's wrong-doing. This approach works best for supervisors, but can be used effectively by peers and associates at times.

Imagine yourself as Paula, the supervisor of Marilee and Roger. Marilee has sat down once again to tell you about Roger's long lunches and late mornings. This time, however, after listening and acknowledging, you do some-thing different—you don't accept the sole responsibility for taking a next step.

"Have you told . . . ?" You might not be able to use Marilee's perceptions of Roger's work in any direct way, but Marilee can. Therefore, the first response from you ought to be, "Have you said to Roger the things you've been saying to me?" If this gets an interested "No, but how would I go about doing this?" you can counsel Marilee and suggest she work up to a private, over-coffee discussion about how she and Roger can work better together. (Don't snicker, I've seen it happen—very oc-casionally.)

"Can I tell . . . ?" If Marilee is like most Triangle Complainers and will not, on her own, deal with Roger directly, say, "Can I tell Roger what you've said about him and that you've said it?" If she says "Yes," you now have particular and concrete issues to bring up to Roger. Your chances of a successful outcome will be far greater than those you would have in a discussion that started, "Roger, I've heard that some people have been having trouble reaching you in the morning." True, Roger can still proclaim innocence, blame others, or rationalize. But it is made more difficult by the impact of "Marilee says that twice she couldn't reach you at 9:00 last week to talk about some mutual cases." More importantly, your ability to work solidly with Roger is unimpaired.

I confess that I don't have much faith that Marilee will say yes. Therefore, here is the next point of interception.

"I'd be happy to . . ." If Marilee will not allow you to quote her to Roger, I believe a variant of point one is indicated: "Well, I can see that you're reluctant to start off a discussion with Roger on your own, but I'd be willing to set one up and to meet with the two of you to work things out."

If Marilee's answer is "Okay," you proceed with a plan for the meeting. Your role should be that of a third party consultant doing the following: assisting each to listen to, understand, and acknowledge the other's messages; helping to define problems; helping to search for solutions. As supervisor, you can insist that they find *some* solution to the problem. However, you should avoid the role of a judging father, whose decision can later be sabotaged. After the third or so meeting they may have worked things out, or at least Marilee won't complain to *you* anymore.

If Marilee's answer is "No," it is important that your reply be, "Well, if you change your mind, let me know." This leaves the ball in her hands, not yours, making it much more difficult for her to complain to you. Nothing in this approach interferes with your right to do further investigating on your own and to obtain any facts that might lead to a productive supervisory meeting with Roger.

WHEN YOU'RE NOT THE BOSS

It's uncomfortable and even depressing to be the target of the badmouthing of one associate by another. The proper reactions are known to most people. It's the doing that is difficult.

If you agree with Sam when he tells you what a lazy person Rex is, your problem is mainly one of how much time you can spend listening to gossip. It will certainly be a very satisfying activity. You will feel superior to Rex because he's lazy and superior to Sam because he's a gossip. All at no cost to your own sense of integrity, since you are merely reaffirming your own perception of Rex. If Rex is a serious enough problem, you might try to turn your agreement into a platform for action by asking Sam, "What should and can we *do* about Rex?" Surprisingly, a plan of action may even result.

I was a member of a volunteer group with a very ineffective, but much liked, leader. After several months of mutual complaining among the group, one person asked, "Well, what are we going to *do* about it?" After a small but uncomfortable silence, we embarked on a positive discussion. The result was the formation of a "carry the bad news" committee that faced the older leader with the need for a "different approach" and developed for their old friend an honorary, face-saving role to play. The difficult task is to move beyond the complacency that mutual complaining can generate into action that forces everyone to deal with the complexities of the situation—not nearly so satisfying an occupation.

When you do *not* agree with Sam that Rex is lazy, your way is also clear but difficult. To sit silent, seeming to agree by your silence, is a self-diminishing act. Yet most of us do it all too frequently because we don't want to risk an open confrontation or the loss of that warm feeling of group cohesiveness. And what harm is there in a few derogatory words that, after all, Rex will never hear? The harms, of course, are several. Each time Rex is called lazy without rebuttal, Sam is affirmed in his perception. He may relay his negative view to others, using your "agreement" as supportive evidence. Out of regard for Rex, you might tell him what Sam has been saying. This transfers the hot potato to Rex in a form that he can neither swallow nor readily spit out. A possible, even probable, danger is that Rex will rush off to an angry confrontation with Sam, only to have Sam deny any intentional slur. Sam then feels traduced and Rex feels frustrated and dumb. A further danger is that your own sense of having failed yourself, as well as Rex, will lead you, doubtless with plausible rationalizations, gradually to find it more comfortable to avoid him. After all, if it weren't for Rex, you wouldn't have been involved in this.

I believe that your job, when you don't agree with the Complainer, is twofold: to refuse to assent by silence; and to balance publicly Sam's negative view with your own positive opinion. By doing the latter, you may prevent the acceptance of Sam's opinion as fact by those who do not know Rex. In addition, you will be able to maintain your own relationship with Rex on a solid basis. In addition, If Rex knows that Sam's statement did not stand alone, his impulse to precipitate action may be easier to control.

The technique is to disagree with Sam's opinion without arguing that he is wrong. You are likely to accomplish little by trying to convince Sam that his view of Rex is incorrect. By challenging him, you increase the tension in an already uncomfortable situation at little gain. Furthermore, for all you know, Rex may have *been* lazy in his dealings with Sam or, at least, he may have done some things, leaving a little early each day, say, that

Sam has interpreted as meaning "lazy." If your differing opinion raises doubts in Sam about the validity of his own, well and good. However, I suggest that you are on shaky grounds if you try to convince Sam that you are right about Rex and that he is wrong.

State your disagreement as soon as you can get it in. As with any situation in which "no" must be said, a delay in doing so increases the level of social discomfort. It will certainly be easier to keep it neutral if you can follow Sam's statement with your own. Nevertheless, if the right moment has passed you by and you were not able to get your courage up until everyone is about to leave, jump in anyway. An "Oh, by the way, I've found Rex to be a very hard worker" shouted after Sam, who is walking down the hall, may not be the best, but it is better than nothing.

To be realistic about this, your goal is to refute Sam with a minimum cost to yourself. If the cost gets too great, you may do nothing. Therefore, keep the situation as informal as you can. "It's really interesting, Sam, that you and I have had such different experiences with Rex. I worked with him quite a bit on that Renfrew project and he never missed a deadline. Worked a lot of nights, too." If Rex is someone you have not yet met, "I'll be interested in seeing if I agree with you about Rex when I meet him" will do.

Finally, if you can, when suggesting an alternate view of Rex, report specific and concrete observations rather than generalized statements such as "Rex is really a good guy."

REVIEW OF COPING WITH COMPLAINERS

—Listen attentively to their complaints even if you feel guilty or impatient.
—Acknowledge what they're saying by paraphrasing and checking out your perception of how they feel about it.
—Don't agree with or apologize for their allegations even if, at the moment, you accept them as true.
—Avoid the accusation-defense-reaccusation pattern.
—State and acknowledge facts without comment.
—Try to move to a problem-solving mode by:
    asking specific, informational questions.
    assigning limited fact-finding tasks.

asking for the complaints in writing, but be serious and
supportive about it.
—If all else fails, ask the Complainer: "How do you want
this discussion to end?"

Chapter 4

CLAMMING UP: THE SILENT AND UNRESPONSIVE PERSON

Helen had just finished her presentation to the executives
of an agency that she hoped would soon be a major
client for her new firm. She had enthusiastically described
and explained the many valuable services she and her
colleagues could provide. With confidence in a job well
done, she had brought her talk to a close with, "Now
have you any comments or questions, gentlemen?" It took
only a few seconds for her to realize that she was in for
a disaster. No interested, enthusiastic response. Not even
any argument. Just three sets of eyes staring—one set at
her, one set at the table, and one set out the window. As
the silence stretched on, she felt her confidence slip away.
"Uh, was there anything that I could clarify?" she lamely
tried.

"Do you suppose you could park your car more on your
side of the driveway," Tom asked his neighbor. "We're
having a little trouble opening our doors." No response.
Tom continued: "Well, I realize there's no real dividing
line, but since we share the same driveway, I've always
envisioned the line down the middle." Still silence from
neighbor Ed, intently polishing his car. "Well," Tom
sighed as he turned to go up his front steps, "I guess we
could just get out on the other side of the car . . ."

THE BEHAVIOR

You've made a statement or asked a question. You expect a reasonable and relevant response. What you get,

however, is a yep, a nope, maybe a grunt, most likely nothing. Unresponsive people are those who clam up just at those times when you need an answer or want some conversation. These Clams, like their bivalve namesakes, react to a probe, a troublesome foreign body, in fact any disagreeable situation, by closing down. Having to do business with these Difficult People may not be as unpleasant as confronting a Sniper or an expert Complainer, but it can be even more maddening.

Not all quiet folks are Clams. Some people don't speak up because they are wise enough to know that they have nothing sensible to say. Others are experts at screening out data that are irrelevant to their purposes; they put you into limbo even while you are speaking. Still others are temporarily quiet because they are intently listening to the conversation and will in fact join in when they have something to say.

What sets Clams apart from these folks? Unfortunately, there is no readily discernible behavioral trait, such as the accusatory style of the Complainer, that differentiates Clams from their merely quiet counterparts. Just plain quiet folks usually don't go out of their way to avoid answering direct questions, like neighbor Ed, however, and they're likely to acknowledge, if asked, that they don't feel they have anything to contribute to a meeting. Beyond that, as we'll see, it's often difficult to tell Clams from non-Clams until you've tried to draw them out.

UNDERSTANDING THE BEHAVIOR

The perplexing thing about Clams is that there are so many varieties of them. All of them, however, learned unresponsiveness in general because it provides a number of short-run benefits. Here are some of the ways that silence works for Clams of various species.

For some species, unresponsiveness is a noncommittal way of handling potentially painful interpersonal situations. If I admit that I used the postage meter for all my overseas Christmas packages, you will yell at me. If I lie, I'll feel guilty. If I say nothing, however, odds are that you will either do all the talking or go away.

For other unresponsive people, the charm of silence is calculated aggression. If you desire to hurt or control people who want or need communication from you, nothing quite matches in finesse and general safety the obviously purposeful withholding of your part in the conversation. Watch as their frustration mounts, as dignity and aplomb fall away in the face of your stonyfaced stare. As an aesthetic experience it's hard to beat.

And, for some, clamming up is a way of evading themselves. Spoken words give concrete reality to thoughts and feelings. To articulate to another, or to yourself, secret fears or aspirations is to face the fact that you have them. How much safer to keep the words safely unspoken, to mask it all by feeling confused, and to skirt the whole issue by remaining close-lipped, letting others fill the silence.

Given this array of motivation, how do you tell what it means? Most of us, asked to speculate about someone else's silence, search our own experience and guess that it masks fear, sullen anger, or spiteful refusal to cooperate. However, as with any nonverbal communication, silence means different things at different times with different people. To figure out what is meant in any particular situation, we go on to seek clues in the Clam's other forms of nonverbal communication.

There are two basic types of nonverbal signs, those of the finger type and those of the frown type. Nonverbals of the finger type—that set of symbolic, stylized actions that we use as we do words, as signs or symbols with standardized meanings—provide relatively easy-to-read clues. If I shake my fist at you, without a smile, do you doubt that I'm sore at you? There is a wide variety of finger, hand, and arm gestures, body stances, or ways and places to touch people, which we use for such purposeful communication. Although gestures, like words, may be misinterpreted, they usually are not.

The second category of nonverbals lacks an intentional quality. It includes that very large number of physiologic and anatomic reactions that accompany any inner emotional state; some of these reactions you notice in yourself, most you are completely oblivious to. To those who notice them, these reactions often have a considerable, if confusing, import. For example, Sergeant Peterson described the nonverbals of his superior of eight months:

When I'm having a discussion with my watch lieutenant about a problem in my unit, I've learned to keep an eye on him. He will suddenly freeze—I mean he becomes a statue. Then his forehead wrinkles up, his mouth turns down, and his face gets red as a beet. I don't mean he stops talking. He goes right on, as if nothing happened. So far, I've run across three reasons for this reaction. He's either disapproving of something I've done, he's got an idea about how to solve the problem, or he's remembered something he forgot to do.

Shaking fists, upraised middle fingers, or smiles in a bar can usually be pretty well read by anyone brought up in our society. Wrinkled foreheads and red faces present a much more difficult problem. For one person they mean "I'm startled," for another, "I'm furious," and for yet another, "I'm thinking." Even more confusing can be the fact that in the same person a wrinkled forehead and a grim expression may accompany both anger *and* intense thought.

Nonverbal clues, then, are seldom sufficient to deduce the nature of the silent beast you're confronting. It's extremely unwise just to guess what is going on inside a Silent and Unresponsive person, because if your guess is wrong, you can create problems that didn't exist before. If you treat a person who is timid as if he or she were angry, you may create your own Difficult Person. Thus, most of the coping steps in the section that follows are designed to get your Clam to open up.

CLAMS IN REVIEW

—Clams are silent, unresponsive people who won't or can't talk when you need conversation from them.
—It is often difficult to understand what the silence or lack of response means.
—Therefore, your major coping task is to get them to talk.

COPING WITH CLAMS

Imagine yourself a supervisor sitting down with Rita for the annual performance review (yes, of course, it should be done more frequently, but it isn't). You begin by telling her a few things, good and bad, that you have observed about her. Having done this, you are ready for a conversation. You'd like to get Rita's viewpoint. Does she agree with your assessment? Does she have any ideas on improving her own performance? These are reasonable things to expect. What you get, however, is nothing. She sits, stares at the floor, softly drumming her fingers on the arm of her chair. So you wonder: Is she angry? Is she controlling you or hurting you as a silent Sniper? Maybe she's worried about her job. Maybe she's just a person with nothing to say. Maybe this, maybe that, maybe anything. Whatever the reasons for her silence, to cope effectively you must find out more. The only way to do that is to get that Clam to talk.

Ask Open-Ended Questions.

The obvious way to get someone to talk is to ask them questions. You might end your initial statement to Rita with "Do you agree?" "Do you have anything to add?" or "Shall I go on?" All of these are reasonable questions to ask. But they won't work with a Clam, because they are all "close-ended," that is, they can be answered with a yes or no, spoken or silent.

To encourage a Clam to open up, you must ask "open-ended" questions, questions that can't properly be answered with a single word or a nod. The open-ended questions to ask Rita would be ones like: "What's your reaction, thus far?" "How do you react to that?" "What are some things that occur to you right now?" Helen, the speaker in the opening anecdote, would have had a much better chance of getting some feedback from those agency executives if she had asked similar questions rather than the close-ended silence makers she used. A highly experienced Clam *can* remain unresponsive when asked an open-ended question, but it does require considerable effort to do so.

Use the Friendly, Silent Stare.

Open-ended questions are particularly effective when they are accompanied by a stance that I've heard characterized as the "friendly, silent stare," or FSS. The FSS calls for a quizzical, expectant expression on your face, eyebrows raised, eyes wide (don't laugh, it really works). If it is natural for you, a slight smile can serve as an invitation to the timid. Some people—those whose silence does mask fear, for example—interpret direct eye contact as a push or even a demand. For this reason, I prefer to center my eyes on a neutral area, such as the lips or the chin. In any case, your visage should communicate an expectation that the Clam will begin to speak any second.

Friendly, silent staring accomplishes three things: (1) It provides a quiet time for collecting thoughts. (2) It gives you something to do and think about while you are waiting for the Clam to open up. (3) It sets the stage for using the leverage that your silence provides.

To be effective, you should generally expect to maintain your friendly, silent stare past the point of your own comfort, unless you happen to be somewhat of a Clam yourself. Some people find themselves growing quite uneasy when silence hangs in the air. This is partly due to the fact that the length of a protracted silence (or to be more exact, the protracted length of a silence) is often hard to judge. You may find it helpful to learn and use the technique of counting time, silently saying to yourself "thousand and one, thousand and two," and so on. For one thing, this gives you something to do while you're sitting there looking alert and expectant. Knowing that it has been only forty seconds since the silence started helps to stand it.

It is especially important, however, to restrain the impulse to out-wait the Clam and thus win the contest. When you become aware that *you* feel the pull of "who can outlast whom," move on to the next coping step.

Don't Fill the Space.

Clams learned to shut up when the going was tough precisely because someone else always rescued them by talking. Whether it was yelling, lecturing, or polite chit-chat, someone else's speech saved them from having to take the initiative in whatever uncomfortable situation they were facing. At all costs, don't reinforce that pattern by ending the silence and returning to the substance of your "conversation." You'll only get deeper into the mire if you pop back in with, "Okay, uh, well now, uh, Rita, how have you been making out with the new bookkeeping system? Are you getting the information that you need?" Expect to feel like doing just this. We were all taught to ease embarrassing situations when we could. Your awareness will make it easier to resist. It also helps to have an alternative response, and you will.

Comment on What's Happening.

Consider what's been happening. You started a conversation at an appropriate time, about a relevant subject. You've received from the Clam no response. You've allowed time, you've looked receptive and expectant, still nothing. To such a crazy situation you must make the only sane response possible: Take a figurative step to one side and comment on the peculiar goings-on. This would have been the best tack for Tom to take in dealing with his silent neighbor Ed. At times it's possible to do this with nothing more than a quizzical look and a questioning gesture. More often you need to put it explicitly: "I expected you to say something, Rita, and you're not. What does it mean?" Notice that you've finished with an open-ended question. You return to your friendly, silent stare and maintain it, calmly interested and expecting a response.

Recycle If Necessary.

If your "what's happening?" comment is met by further silence, hold your own quiet waiting for as long as you can stand it and then recomment: "Well, to me it looks like this is what's going on: I'm waiting for your reaction and you're not saying anything. How do we get out of this bind?" If you can keep it in mind, always try to end with an open-ended question and a return to expectant waiting.

As the pressure builds, *or* when contentious Clams believe that you've been well disposed of, you may be hit with a version of "Can I go now?" ("I've gotta go now" is the usual variant when you're not in charge.) When this happens, use a reasonably strong yet nonprovoking reply that allows you to maintain control of the conversation. "Not yet, I still have some things on my mind."

Help Break the Tension.

At this point, it's worth trying again to help the Clam begin. Everyone at times has trouble being articulate. This is especially true when feelings, confusions, or complex thoughts need to be expressed. Here are some questions and statements that can often help another person get started.

(1) "Can you talk about what makes it difficult to say what you're thinking?"
(2) "Are you concerned about my reaction to what you'd like to say? How do you think I'll react?"
(3) "What's the thought?"
(4) "What's the conflict?"
(5) "You look distressed."
(6) "Don't worry about starting at the beginning, what's on your mind right now?"
(7) "Am I wrong that you're feeling uncomfortable [or irritated, annoyed, or impatient]?" (I often use this convoluted question form because it seems to have a disarming quality.)

The last question assumes that you might be in error about the meaning of whatever signs have led to your perception. Be ready for a "Yes, you are wrong." Be further ready to accept it. The temptation can be great to say, "Yes, you are, too," to someone who, with clenched fists and red face, says, "No, I'm not angry." Here are two reasons for resisting that temptation.

Some people are not every aware of how they're feeling at the moment. Later, they may vaguely realize, "I must have been angry," but at the time, the focus of their attention is elsewhere. To insist that they are angry when they don't feel angry is futile. Even so, it can be useful to come back with, "Oh, when I saw your forehead wrinkle, I wondered if I'd pushed the wrong button."

The second reason for simply accepting your Clam's assertion is to avoid being caught at the receiving end of a controlled conversation. If I, the Clam, can successfully pull you into an argument about how I'm feeling, I can't lose. I am the only final arbiter, and you will look, and feel, faintly ridiculous if you try to tell me what's going on in my mind.

Accepting the answer doesn't mean you should let the budding conversation drop, however. Let the reply be a signal for you to press on: "Well, if you aren't angry, what is the problem?" or "Since you're not angry, what were your reasons for not letting me know that your division was no longer handling customer complaints?"

Set Time Limits.

If you know in advance that you will be dealing with a Clam, plan out how much time you should spend on this character. If you believe the relationship important, and the subject relevant to your own needs, you'll be wise to set aside enough time for adequate coping. After all, if you're fidgety because an important client is waiting, you are not likely to do a good job of being calm.

There are three important reasons to establish definite time limits when dealing with Clams. First, you will be better able to remain quietly waiting if necessary, because you know you have reserved a half hour (or fifteen minutes or two hours). Second, the silence you're encountering may be the result of ambivalence about whether or not a sensitive topic should be brought up. Well known to counselors or therapists is the fact that important topics are often saved until the last ten minutes of the allotted time. A time limit may help to energize your Clam to spit out whatever it is that's so difficult to say. Finally, if you have an ending time in mind, you'll know when to move to the last coping step.

When the Clam Answers "I Don't Know."

If you come up against a skillful, hard-playing Clam, expect your open-ended questions to receive an almost unbeatable reply: "I don't know." Visualize the possibilities: "How do you react thus far?" "I don't know." "What's happening?" "I don't know." "What's on your mind right now?" "I don't know." And so forth.

These tactics sometimes work in eliciting a more productive answer:

(1) Assume that the "I don't know" is a genuine response, and try one of the suggestions that assist people in getting unstuck.
(2) Reply "What else?" and stay in your expectant stance. This gives you something to say to decrease your own feeling of tension, but leaves the Clam with the ball.
(3) Treat the "I don't know" as a nonresponse and comment on the fact that your meeting seems to be at an impasse. Then return to your friendly, silent stare.

If these actions, or any others that you can think of on

the spur of the moment, fail, be ready to move on to the last coping step, described on page 66.

WHAT IF YOUR CLAM OPENS?

By this time, you *may* have succeeded in starting a conversation. Here are two points to keep in mind.

Be Attentive When Clams Talk.

If and when an active response comes, pay close attention and use all means possible to demonstrate active listening. Nod your head, paraphrase back what you think you've heard, and don't look at your watch.

If you like to talk and don't like to be in the deep freeze, be careful. When the silence finally ends, and the Clam starts talking, the feeling of relief is so great it can be hard to hold back your own gush of conversation. Remember that the small flame of response that you've been nurturing can easily be blown out.

Let Them Be Oblique.

Frequently, an initial line of response will not seem very relevant to the subject *you* want to discuss. If it is *completely* unrelated—"It's a nice day today" when the topic was "Why didn't Joe get that raise?"—treat it as another kind of nonresponse and stay with your coping process. But if it appears to be a genuine attempt to talk with you about something serious, allow the speaker to continue. It may turn out to be more closely connected than you think. For example, after your opening comments on her performance, Rita may finally speak.

RITA: Well, I haven't been happy with the new bookkeeping system.
YOU: Um. How has it been a problem?
RITA: I can't get any information on travel costs until the end of the month.
YOU: How does that interfere?
RITA: Well, it's one reason I've been overrunning my cost estimation so much [one of the points you've raised].
YOU: I didn't know that was on your mind. Let's talk about what we can do . . .

Even if Rita does not herself reconnect her statements with the matter at hand, you are now in a better position to move on yourself. The pump has been primed and a flow of conversation started. You can bring the discussion back to your topic with: "This is interesting, but could we get back to it at three o'clock? Let's use the time till then to talk further about your work. As I was saying . . ."

WHEN THE CLAM STAYS CLOSED

Let's assume that you've tried all the techniques suggested and nothing has worked. Your Clam remains closed, the subject that needed discussion is still untouched. What is left to do other than be frustrated?

What remains is an old trap to be avoided, and a solid and satisfying ending step to take.

Avoid the Polite Ending.

When the ending time you've agreed upon has arrived, again resist the pull of those niceties you've learned about smoothing over an embarrassing situation. Do not say, "Well, Rita, uh, thanks for coming in, have a nice weekend," or "Okay, Rita, I'll have this typed up and you'll get a copy." Don't stand there awkwardly while Rita silently leaves the room. These are very understandable actions, but they fritter away your remaining chance. You can yet save the day by bringing this baffling interaction to a definite close, while making your Clam realize that he or she will not be let off the hook.

With a subordinate, it might take the following form. You stand and walk toward the door saying, "All right, Rita. It looks as if we just can't get anywhere with this right now. It's an important issue to me and I just can't let it drop. Please see me from 2:00 to 3:00 tomorrow. Check your calendar and call if we need to set another time." You stand by the door and wait for Rita to leave.

If it's your boss, a client, or a customer, you'll undoubtedly need to make adjustments in the approach. "I'll call you tomorrow for an appointment," for example, might sit a little better with these people. What is important is that (1) you initiate the end of the meeting and (2) you indicate your intention to raise the subject again.

Follow Through.

You must, of course, follow through if you expect to make any headway. If you cancel Rita's two o'clock appointment or "forget" to call your customer, you will have wasted the important, if yet uncapitalized-on, gains from your previous coping efforts. When that follow-up meeting does take place, you will be set to proceed through whatever coping steps are necessary to break through.

Interestingly enough, a positive and direct ending to a nondiscussion may produce the very reaction you've been trying for all along. Sometimes even more than you've bargained for. These are some responses I've received:

> Just a minute, you! I've been sitting here so angry I was afraid if I said anything, I'd throw something.

> What? What? No, wait a sec, Dr. Bramson. I've been sitting here thinking about what you said about my being late. It reminded me of something my wife said last night. [This after fifteen minutes of my asking open-ended questions and he nodding "interestedly" and looking me square in the eye.]

> Why do you have to keep picking on me? Let me alone.

Each of these responses led to valuable discussions at a follow-up meeting. Tempting as it may be to continue once the door has been opened, I believe that you gain more in the long run by acknowledging the message and the feeling behind it, yet sticking to the time limit. This advice does not preclude negotiating a new ending time, if your own schedule will permit it.

At Length, Proceed on Your Own.

You have gone to the mat with that Clam as many times as you can, all to no avail. Your boss still will not discuss that official reprimand he put in your file. Rita will not talk about her sloppy work. At this point there is little left to do but simply report to your nemesis the steps you plan to take, given the impossibility of a real discussion.

Since we can't seem to work this out, Rita, here's what I need to do to satisfy myself. First, I'm going to dictate a memo to you with a copy to the file outlining what I've been saying about your performance. I will expect a reply. If you do not reply, I will assume you agree with my analysis and will so note in your file. I intend to meet with you every Tuesday for the next three months to check on your progress. If your error count doesn't improve by March 31, I'll have to send a termination notice to you. . . .

By this time, you will have made some assumption about what the lack of response means. Make those assumptions as explicit as you can. For example:

Mr. Williams, I am assuming that your silence [or unwillingness to talk about the reprimand you put in my file] means that you disagree with my view that my refusal to change the wording of that memo was not insubordination. On that basis, I am filing a grievance.

There are two reasons for making this assumption explicit. An "I assume your silence means you agree" can, even at this last ditch, pull out a response that will lead somewhere. In addition, you help yourself relinquish remaining doubts about your interpretation of the unresponsiveness. This allows you to be resolute in taking whatever steps you must to remedy the situation.

REVIEW OF COPING WITH CLAMS

—Rather than trying to interpret what the silence means, get the Clam to open up.
—Ask open-ended questions.
—Wait as calmly as you can for a response. Use counseling questions to help reticent Clams.
—Do not fill in the silence with your conversation.
—Plan enough time to allow you to wait with composure.
—Get agreement on or state clearly how much time is set aside for your "conversation."
—If you get no response, comment on what's happening. End your comment with an open-ended question.
—Again, wait as long as you can, then:
comment on what's happening and wait again.

try to keep control of the interaction by dealing matter-
of-factly with "Can I go now?" and "I don't know"
responses.
—When the Clam opens up:
  be attentive and watch your own impulse to gush.
  flow with tangential comments. They may lead to some-
    thing relevant and important. If they don't, state your
    own need to return to the original topic.
—If the Clam stays closed:
  avoid a polite ending.
  terminate the meeting yourself and set up another ap-
    pointment.
  at length, inform the Clam what you must and will do,
    since a discussion has not occurred.

Chapter 5

SUPER-AGREEABLES AND OTHER WONDERFULLY NICE PEOPLE

Man, am I pissed. Last month I spent three hours setting up an aisle display at Matthews Drugs in Kingston.
Joe Matthews was so happy with it he took me out for
a drink afterward and told me how he really liked the
way our company was treating him—he bought the
whole promotion without a question. I can hear him
now: "Pete, I just need to get my books up to date and
I'll make you the hero of your district—I mean a *big*
order." Today the month-end summary came out and
that S.O.B. Matthews has cut his order by 30 percent.
Now I have a down month, no bonus, and to top it
all, I let some other customers go to give him the
extra time.

THE BEHAVIOR

Poor Pete. How could someone as wonderful, as
friendly, and as compliant as Joe Matthews ever be a
problem to anyone? People like Joe always have a smile
and a friendly word for you. Best of all, they seem so
responsive. Whatever you want from them, you get. What
neat, sweet people, UNTIL you need some action: that

order form *signed,* your raise approved *in writing,* an honest and tough-minded discussion of a problem. How do you fight someone who always agrees with you? Without a clear path to your goal, without concrete obstacles to hurdle, what is there left but to feel your blood pressure rise as you become more and more mired in super-agreeableness?

Super-Agreeables always tell you things that are satisfying to hear. They are Difficult People precisely because they leave you believing they are in agreement with your plans, only to let you down. Super-Agreeables are outgoing people, sociable, and personal with others in a way that makes for friendly interactions. "Bill Perry, was that the name? Hi! My name's Carleton Cramer. Say, don't I remember you from the newspapers? Weren't you on the high school football team? No? Funny, you look just like that great halfback they had in 1967." Like Carleton Cramer, they may not pay close attention to what you're saying, but they are very attentive to *you.*

Super-Agreeables often use humor as a way to ease a conversation. The humor may have a joshing quality, but it's chiefly intended as an expression of intimacy rather than as a dig. "Hi, Mary! Still leaving the family to fend for itself, I see. I'm so glad you could make the meeting." Sometimes, however, Super-Agreeables do use humor as a way of sending serious messages, as we'll see in a moment.

UNDERSTANDING THE BEHAVIOR

To be liked and loved by others is a need common to all of us. Who hasn't felt a glow from words, looks, or that arm around the shoulder that said, "I like you, you're okay with me." For most of us, most of the time, the need for the personal affirmation that we are indeed likeable takes its place among the other interpersonal needs common to human beings. We find a balance point that integrates our needs to do a job well and to find a reasonable place in the pecking order with a reasonable concern for being liked.

The burden with which Super-Agreeables are saddled is that their balance point is so far to one extreme that they need to be liked or at least accepted by every single person all of the time. For this type of Difficult Person, the catastrophe to be prevented or evaded whenever possible is open conflict, with its terrifying possibility that acceptance, approval or love will be withdrawn.

Satisfying such an overwhelming need to be liked appears so futile that some people abandon the quest and isolate themselves. For them, loneliness is more tolerable than the constant threat of rejection. For those stuck with the need to be liked but without the knack for gaining continual affirmation, separation, whether physical or psychological, may be the only liveable alternative. Super-Agreeables, however, have the knack and bring it to bear with telling effect.

Some folks discover, often very early in life, a fail-safe method for getting instant affection. Here's the "secret": People like people who have the good sense to like them. If we should meet at a party and I should smile in a way that leaves you *feeling* accepted, won't you surely (unless the research on interpersonal attractions is all wrong) feel good about me? Then, in a dozen subtle ways, won't you let me know that you like me, too?

To have made this insight second nature and to be skillful at using it—what a godsend for one who needs approval. Whether at seven years old ("Gee, Mom, you make the best chocolate chip cookies in the world") or at thirty ("Well, all reet! Am I glad to see you, friend"), it works and works and works.

If life were simple and conflict-free, Super-Agreeables would hardly ever be Difficult People. But adult activities are usually complex. They involve work to be done, social niches to be won, and fun to be had, sometimes all at the same time, and these intertwined needs generate conflict—just what Super-Agreeables desperately want to avoid.

And they do avoid it, at least for a time. Because they are ever reluctant to interpose between themselves and others any hint that they might not always be good fellows, Super-Agreeables often make unrealistic commitments: "I'll have that report for Thursday morning," "I'll get a check in the mail right away," "Your car will be ready at 4:30 sharp," or "I'll be home in fifteen minutes," said with such sincerity and good will that belief is generated, even in those who have believed and then been let down many times before.

These promises are often made in good faith by the Super-Agreeables. That confident promise, "I'll be home in fifteen minutes," made in the face of terrible traffic conditions that guarantee it will be a thirty-minute trip, makes sense when viewed from a Super-Agreeable perspective. If you could hear, as they do, the wish in your own voice that they be home as soon as possible, you might understand why the reality of traffic can't be allowed to keep them from being what you want. If it means giving you pie in the sky, at the moment, so be it.

Like other Difficult Person situations I've described, the Super-Agreeable's avoidance of conflict has some short-term benefits, but these are gained at a long-term high cost. Joe Matthews, for example, simply handled conflict the way over-agreeable people usually do. He told Pete everything nice that he wanted to hear, but avoided some not-so-nice truths. Joe had simply kept to himself the facts that he had recently decided to upgrade and expand his cosmetics department and that he had already ordered heavily from a manufacturer with an "exclusive" name and a costlier line. For Joe, the problem was: "If I tell Pete what I'm really thinking, he'll be upset and angry with me. But if I order from his company, too, my cash position will be terrible. Besides that, I'll have to cut back on his order sometime." He tried to resolve this problem by being extra nice to Pete while cutting his company's order. The benefit of this course for Joe was that he didn't have to face directly the loss of Pete's approval. Pete gained, too: he felt great—for a while. The longer-term costs for both parties out-weighed these benefits, however. Pete wasted precious time and now feels traduced by Joe; Joe realizes that he's made Pete angry but will be triply nice and even less truthful next time; Pete will start to avoid making calls on Joe and will get yelled at by his boss.

The tragedy is that if Super-Agreeables were straightforward to begin with, and they and you could put up with some minor unpleasantries, the problem could more easily be resolved and much bad feeling could be avoided. If Pete, for instance, had only known about Joe Matthews' decision to upgrade his cosmetics department:

(1) He would not have spent so much valuable time on a marginally productive display.

(2) The display could have emphasized the company's more luxurious products. Ironically, Pete had built his colorful display around highly advertised, lower-priced items.

(3) Pete would not have been so disappointed; he could have given the bad news to his boss rather than having it show up in the monthly statistics.

(4) Joe and he could continue to have a productive relationship, informed by an understanding of each other's needs.

SUPER-AGREEABLES IN REVIEW

—Super-Agreeables have strong needs to be liked and accepted.

—Because it is a useful method for gaining acceptance, they make others feel liked and approved of.

—They are Difficult People only when their needs to give and receive friendship conflict with negative aspects of reality.

—Rather than directly risk losing your friendship or approval, Super-Agreeables will commit themselves to actions on which they cannot or will not follow through.

COPING WITH SUPER-AGREEABLES

The nature of Super-Agreeable behavior suggests a strategy for coping with it. The Super-Agreeable manipulates the presentation of reality in order to gain your approval. Your strategy is to reassure the Super-Agreeable so that it does not appear to him or her that there is any conflict between spilling the beans and gaining or retaining your approval. This way, the Super-Agreeable is reassured and you get the facts. You need those facts because only issues that come to the surface can be resolved. Hidden problems influence events but are out of your effective control. Here's how to put this strategy into practice.

Make Honesty Nonthreatening.

Although Super-Agreeables *should* be candid with you, they won't be. Even an intention to be open doesn't get them past the urgent necessity to tell you what they think you want to hear. This doesn't mean that you never accept "Wow, what a great job you guys're doing" at face value, enjoying the friendship and warmth that accompanies the praise. When nothing of importance is at stake and you have not yet determined that you are dealing with a Super-Agreeable, there's no problem. But when either of these conditions exists, extending a few helps to honesty can save future aggravation. Here are some steps that have worked.

Many times all that's needed is a straightforward request for an honest opinion, especially when it can be sincerely accompanied by words that say "I really want to know what's on your mind because I value your friendship." The more accepted your Super-Agreeable feels, the less need there is for subterfuge. Most people come to grief with Super-Agreeables because they *don't* ask them to be candid, fearing that the glow from those nice words might be disturbed.

You make it easier for anyone heavily loaded with the over-agreeable quality to speak the truth if you make it clear that their criticism won't earn them your displeasure. For instance, instead of saying, "Well, what *didn't* you like about my report, Sam?" say "I'm really glad you like my report, Sam, but every report has some parts better than others, even if it's all good. Which parts do you think are not up to the best?" For the same reasons that it's easier for a teacher to get parental and student acceptance for giving a "B" grade rather than a "D," Super-Agreeables will find less strain in telling you about what's "good" but not "outstanding" rather than what's "bad." Once again, it can't hurt to add some statement such as "I enjoy working with you so much I don't want anything to interfere with our relationship."

Be Personal—When You Can.

To the extent that you can be "personal" with Super-Agreeables, it helps. By this, I *don't* mean revealing personal secrets, or asking for deep or feeling-laden conversation. Being personal here means bringing up in conversation questions or statements about Super-Agreeable's personal life. For example: "Is that your family in the picture?" "Is that a new tie you're wearing?" "Say, I really like that dress."

By penetrating the formal relationships and work roles

that separate us all, and reaching out with words, you show the Super-Agreeables that you see them as people in whom you are interested. You give them a floor of acceptance upon which to risk straight talk about facts.

If you don't really feel an interest in good old George, however, don't fake it. Super-Agreeables have large and sensitive antennae. They are alert to negative nonverbal signs and, being experts in phoniness themselves, they have a special nose for detecting it in others. (They would make excellent credit checkers, *if* they didn't have to turn anyone down personally.) If your efforts to be personal are forced, or are to conceal your own anger, it will almost certainly be detected. You then will end up with more of what you didn't want in the first place— sweet talk. If you don't feel warm toward George, it's better to let him realize that he has nothing to lose by giving you a straight answer than it is to make him suspicious of your true feelings.

Don't Allow Super-Agreeables to Make Unrealistic Commitments.

It can save everyone a lot of trouble if Super-Agreeables can be prevented from making commitments they won't keep. At least it's worth a try. When the Super-Agreeable says, "I'll be home in fifteen minutes," you say, "Well, okay, but given traffic at this hour, it's taken me about forty-five minutes the last few times. I'll expect you at 6:15. [It's now 5:30.] If you make it earlier, fine." (And don't start looking at the clock at 5:45. No matter what was said, *you* know it will be 6:15.)

When he or she says, "The check'll be in the mail tonight," you don't say, "In a pig's eye it will," but "I know a lot of people have been having trouble getting cash together at this time of year. Is that going to be a problem for you?"

Be Prepared to Compromise.

You may be faced with a situation that requires open conflict with a Super-Agreeable. Where possible, it pays to enter the conflict prepared to negotiate and compromise in order to resolve the problem to your ultimate best advantage. Since Super-Agreeables tend to be most apprehensive in situations in which they are likely to lose the favor of others, they are partial to so-called win-win solutions. These are decisions which, through compromise and negotiation, satisfy some needs of both sides of a controversy. "You'll get some of what you want and I'll get some of what I want, and we'll both be pleased." If you have trouble giving in when you feel you're right, you may want to do some advance thinking and be prepared with something to offer that you *can* give up. Understand, it's not to placate that you do this. It's to reduce tension so that the disagreement can be brought to a realistic resolution. When tension levels get high, Super-Agreeables will agree to results that they will not, or cannot, produce.

It helps to make your compromising move as early as you can. For example, as soon as you're settled, say, "Millie, before we get started, I want to let you know that I've thought over the discussion we had about how often to have our meetings. I still think one a month is enough, but I'm willing to go along wtih every two weeks if that would help." This helps your Super-Agreeable to relax before tension begins to build over the possibility of your conflict.

Listen to Their Humor.

Indirect communication is a way of compromising a conflict over whether to tell the truth or to distort it out of fears of distressing or alienating others. Such communication may even take the form of saying something positive when you're thinking something negative. To give them their due, Super-Agreeables sometimes do use humor in a quite useful way as the bit of sugar that eases a bitter pill down. But more often, they fall back on humor as a way to speak the truth and at the same time belie it.

Double-edged humor is a perfect means of expression for the Super-Agreeable. Suppose I, as a Super-Agreeable, have a problem with you, but I surround it with a joke. I need only keep an eye on you to see how open I can be about my criticism. If you show signs of hurt or anger, I'm in great shape to deny that I meant it. If you don't, I can proceed.

So when you walk up to your Super-Agreeable's office door and get, along with a cheery smile and a wave, "Well, here's old Mr. [or Ms.] Expert again," pay attention. Nothing more than a joyous welcome to someone who can be counted on to know a lot? Sure! Then again, it may be that "knows a lot" has somehow become "knows it all." If the relationship is important, a return visit to check out your Super-Agreeable's real meaning informally and couched in a positive way might be worthwhile. You might say, "Em, over the weekend I was thinking about your calling me 'old Mr. Expert' the other day. At the time I just thought it was funny and kind of nice but I've been wondering. Is there something I'm doing that gets in the way? Working with you has been such a pleasure that I'd hate to let anything spoil it."

Following through like this is the proper thing to do, and the payoff is great, when it works. But my own experience doesn't permit me to have much faith in its success. Don't be surprised if you get a worried denial that it was anything but a joke and much overconcern that your feelings were hurt. When this happens, pushing further is likely to produce only panic and embarrassment. Either let it go with a "Well, I'm glad" or, better yet, an invitation to coffee or lunch. But none of this should keep you from staying alert to how your own future behavior may affect the Super-Agreeable.

COPING WITH SUPER-AGREEABLES IN PRACTICE

Let's see what might have happened differently if Pete had tried some of these coping methods with Joe. My comments are on the right.

PETE: Well, Joe, I am finished. What do you think?

Pete, you're inviting the sugar.

JOE: Saaay, that's fantastic, Pete. I've never seen anything like it. I've been looking over your promo pieces and they're just great!

And you're getting it. (In actuality, according to Pete, this was a monologue that went on for three or four minutes.)

PETE: I'll bet this will increase your orders for stuff by 30 percent the first month. Would it be a good idea to stock up now?

You've muffed your first chance, Pete. This makes it harder for Joe to be honest. He knows that you won't like losing that bonus.

JOE: How about you coming over to Jake's with me for a couple of drinks. I'd like to show my appreciation.

Pretty fancy footwork, Joe.

PETE: I'd never pass up a chance for a drink on you, Joe. But let's hold up a minute. Joe, I really am glad you seem to like the display and the ad stuff. Can we sit down together and go over it in a little more detail; for instance, what really catches your eye, what's okay but not the best? We mean to be around here for a long time and I want to make sure we get plenty of drinks from you.

Helpful as a sign of camaraderie.
Good boy, Pete, you were alert to the sudden distraction.
It's easier to be negative about little pieces than big.

A second personal touch.

JOE: Well, Pete [long pause] —the only little thing that's maybe not quite up to par are the pieces on your "Fifth Avenue" line. I've been getting more than a few customers from Piedmont Estates lately, and of course those exclusive birds wouldn't think of using the same stuff as we mortals. They're really in the market for "eau du snob" or nothing.

Joe tries out a "hat in the door" lead to see how receptive to honesty Pete might be.

PETE: Tell me more, this is just what I want to hear. We'll do better by you, and us, in the long run if we fit in with your needs.

Good response. Keeps it going. Gives permission for negatives.

JOE: Maybe I ought to tell you that I have been talking to some people from that "Angel's Breath" outfit. I'll still keep up your order, of course, but I think I need some really exclusive products, too, to get those folks from the hills into the store. Snobby or not, they've got the bucks.

Joe still can't bring himself to talk about cutting the order.

PETE: Sounds like you've really been thinking this over, Joe. But aren't you going to have some cash flow problems if you maintain the size of your order? Suppose we cut your order 10 percent for next month. We'll change the mix so as to also increase our top lines. Meanwhile, I'll get in touch with our headquarters to see if they have anything else to offer. Maybe we can get you a line as good as Angel's Breath for less . . .

Now Pete can do some problem solving, the main reason for getting the realities surfaced.

Keeps Joe out of trouble and reduces surprises which Pete will have to live with later.

Pete needs restraint here. It is relatively easy to get Super-Agreeables to go along. A little pressure would have pushed Joe into keeping his full order—for this month, that is.

Now, old buddy, how about those drinks?

Keeps the relationship going and rewards Joe's best efforts at being candid.

REVIEW OF COPING WITH SUPER-AGREEABLES

—You must work hard to surface the underlying facts and issues that prevent the Super-Agreeables from taking action.
—Let them know that you value them as people by:
   telling them directly.
   asking or remarking about family, hobbies, wearing apparel. Do this only if you mean it, at least a little.
—Ask them to tell you about those things that might interfere with your good relationship.
—Ask them to talk about any aspect of your product, service, or self (if appropriate, only) that is not as good as the best.
—Be ready to compromise and negotiate if open conflict is in the wind.
—Listen to a Super-Agreeable's humor. There may be hidden messages in those quips or teasing remarks.

Chapter 6

WET BLANKET POWER: THE NEGATIVIST AT WORK

It was four months since Gary Hanning, newly hired with a shiny MBA, had been assigned to troubleshoot with Richard Sheldon, head of the accounting department. He'd had plenty of opportunity to see why the top people had been so concerned over antiquated accounting procedures and why they'd asked him to "see what could be done." But what had promised to be an opportunity for Gary to show his ability as a problem solver had quickly turned into a futile and frustrating experience. Gary described it this way to his wife:

> Can you imagine an insurance company that still reconciles checking accounts by hand? [He moaned.] The place is run so poorly that almost any change would be for the better, but I simply cannot get Dick Sheldon to move. That man has more wet blanket power than anyone I've ever seen. Everything I propose "just won't work." The staff is "resistant," "the techs are untrainable," "they can't be replaced because they're old hands," "it would take too much time to convert to ADP." Every answer is plausible—Dick's no dummy. When I try to find ways to get around these problems, he just says, "We tried that two years ago and it flopped." Then he sits back, sighs, and reaches over to the mountain of forms he has to sign. At the end of four months, my well of ideas has dried up. Maybe he's right, and nothing can be done.

"Well," said his wife, "he's certainly done a good job of dragging you down."

THE BEHAVIOR

People like Dick Sheldon are Negativists—enervating people, often reasonably competent in their own right, who respond to anyone else's productive suggestion with "It won't work" or "It's no use trying" or "We tried that last year" or "Forget it, they'll never let us do it." If you, out of sheer exasperation, should say, "Well, then, what should we do?" you'd better be ready for, "Nothing, there's just no way to deal with that problem. We've tried it before." These conversation-stoppers are said with such conviction that you're likely to begin believing that all your hopes for the future have just been figments of silly over-optimism.

It is important to differentiate Negativists, who dampen any suggestion regardless of merit, from those thoughtful people who, presented with a new proposal, carefully consider the reasons for not taking the given course of action before jumping in. For example, many people who have seen worthy projects fail because no one stopped to ask what might go wrong, use "negative analysis" profitably. This is a practical decision-making method in which you search for unplanned effects that might result from a given course of action. After these possible disasters have been identified, you then plan ways to evade, overcome, or minimize these effects. What differentiates between productive contingency planners and Negativists is that movement from the statement of the problem to "Therefore, here's what we'd better do"—a tack that is anathema to the Negativist. In practice it's fairly easy to tell these breeds apart. In response to an emphatic statement such as, "But if we buy that new pick-up our credit will be way overextended," say, "Well, that's a good point—is there some way around that problem?" Listen to what follows. If it's "Maybe we could manage with a used one," you can relax. If, by contrast, you hear, "There's nothing we can do," then you have a Negativist on your hands.

Negativists often have a profoundly detrimental impact on work groups. It is easy to underestimate this impact because most of us know that obstacles can often be collectively overcome. When the conditions are right, problems stimulate our search for alternatives rather than discourage them. But when a skilled Negativist is at work, the effect is quite different. Here is a sample.

A social service staff was meeting to try to work on some long-standing problems. I had been asked to sit in by upper-level management to facilitate the process and suggest alternatives, because they believed, correctly, that morale was low. The first and, as it turned out, the only issue touched upon was how the staff could get more space. The problem seemed real enough: four or five desks crowded into each small office, no privacy, a small, cold, and drab room for interviewing. The discussion went like this:

VIRGINIA (the supervisor): "We've been complaining about this problem for months. What can we do about it?"

STAN: "I can't believe that Turner [the agency head] would allow this situation to continue. He must know that we can't do any more than fill out forms here."

DON: "And that in the face of a training program on counseling skills. It's impossible."

VIRGINIA: "Well, I've told Dieter [her boss] about the problem and how unhappy everyone is, but he says that everyone is short of space."

BRAMSON: "Is it certain that Mr. Turner understands the consequences of your lack of space?"

VIRGINIA: "Well, he must know that . . ."

DON (interrupting): "There's just no sense going on this way. Those people know what we need, they are not going to help us to do anything, so let's forget it."

MAUDE: "Wait a minute. I want to hear what Virginia was going to say."

VIRGINIA (with a sigh): "Well, maybe Don's right. I mentioned it to Dieter over and over again."

BRAMSON: "I'm sure that it's been discouraging. Sometimes, though, people don't pay the same attention to complaints that they pay to a written list of costs in time, money . . ."

VIRGINIA: "Well, I guess we haven't really . . ."

DON (interrupting): "It won't do any good. Has Turner ever come around here, except to breeze through the halls? They're too busy playing politics to care."

STAN: "Don's right. Let's go on to something else."

MAUDE: "But . . . oh, all right."

VIRGINIA: "What are we going to do about getting more foster home placements?"

DON: "We're not going to do anything until we get the Board to raise compensation rates . . ."

Silence.

Even as I take this dialogue from my notes, I feel again that depressed, bogged-down atmosphere. Individually, everyone had looked forward to the meeting. Their expectations were high. Yet disappointment and feelings of helplessness, rather than action plans, were the sad result.

UNDERSTANDING THE BEHAVIOR

Negativists are able to gain such power over others because they tap that potential for despair in each of us. We have all felt victim to forces beyond our control. Bureaucracies are huge and can seem inflexible. Accidents and illness void carefully made plans. "The world is great and fate conspires" is an accurate, if partial, description of anyone's life. All of us, therefore, can feel angry helplessness when the negative realities in a situation are pointed out in a way that communicates discouragement. Because Negativists truly *feel* dispirited and defeated, their pessimistic comments can easily arouse resonant feelings in friends, family, or colleagues.

To understand Negativists, it is important to realize that they are not by intention obstructionists to every scheme. They, in truth, believe that the blocking forces are out of their, or any ordinary person's, control. No one in the group wanted the space crush alleviated more than Don, for example. To him, however, the negatives he saw were real and decisive. He had, in truth, written complaining memos to headquarters with no response. The big boss *was* busy and made no planned visits to the service unit staff meetings. Such resistant forces that need to be overcome or evaded are ever present. If that were not the case, there would never be any problems. To a Negativist, however, these forces are absolute, immutable barriers, rather than obstacles that one just *might* go around, through, or over.

Negativists, like Complainers, are convinced that they have little power over their own lives. Fate, in the form of overpowering natural or manmade forces, intervenes at every front, never completely within anyone's power to contain. While this view is tempered for most of us by the realization we always have some power to affect our lives, even at times substantial amounts, for the Negativists, with so little belief in their ability to influence things, only trust in others, or hope that fate will deal kindly, is available.

But what if one believes that those who have power cannot be trusted, or, even worse, what if they cannot be counted upon to act reasonably and consistently? Then there remains nothing left but angry, resentful acceptance.

This is the lot of Negativists, and it is what separates them from Complainers, who do not as often possess this embittered quality. Negativists are people who, in their developing years, were unable to work through a basic human disappointment.

We all, to some reasonable degree, have had to come to terms with an unpalatable realization: our parents are not gods or goddesses, nor even demons; they are just ordinary, very real but also fallible people.

To any child, this is a frightening and bitter notion. Facing it is accompanied by angry storms, the loneliest of fears, and great disappointment. After all, if "they" make mistakes and don't know what they're doing, I will have to take care of *myself*. Or at least face the fact that to be cared for by others, since they don't owe it to me as a birthright, I'll have to care for them, too. So scary is this realization that most of us, even if we don't think about it much, hang on tightly to a bit of magical belief —that, to paraphrase sociologist Ida Hoos, *"somewhere* there must be grownups around who know what's going on."* Negativists drag us down so easily because most of us have at least remnants of the strong emotions that once filled that well of deep disappointment. Oh, parents, why have you failed us so? Can no one be trusted?

If there is a little of this cosmic bitterness in all of us, there is a lot in those few that become Negativists. To be sure, they are not aware of this underlying loss of faith in the future. They see instead a constant flow of reasons why life events cannot be dealt with in a positive way. To make sense of this pessimistic view, they support it with the best rationality they can muster. They are no different from the rest of us in needing to validate their deeply held concepts through the evidence of their own senses. Having done that, they state the same perspective with that conviction that comes from a deep belief. Small wonder that they become irritated with you when you persist in thinking that something might yet be done to save the situation.

NEGATIVISTS IN REVIEW

—Negativists are people who, while at times personally capable, have a deep-seated conviction that any task not in their own hands will fail.

—Their negativism is elicited by others' attempts to solve
a problem or improve a procedure.

—Because they believe that others in power don't care
or are self-serving, their negative statements are made
with conviction.

COPING WITH NEGATIVISTS

Avoid Getting Drawn In.

Negativists, with their steadfast, rational communication
of helpless resentment, can touch that potential for depression in each of us and induce in us that same sense
of being blunted. Recognition of your own vulnerability
to discouragement can help you avoid being drawn into
an underlying purpose of negative behavior—gaining confirmation from others that the situation is indeed hopeless.
After all, it is nice to have the company of others who
agree that nothing can be done. For Negativists, that
collective depression affirms the central meaning that
they have given to their own lives.

I have observed problem-solving groups reduced to
absolute silence because they have allowed themselves
to be sucked into the Negativist world view. They sit
staring at the floor, baffled by a negativistic person who
has firmly and repeatedly announced, "There's just no
sense trying, he'll never let it happen." "He," of course,
is the big boss. "Those people don't want us to be able
to solve this problem." "They have reasons of their own
and there's just no point in doing anything." "It'll never
work; don't you remember, we tried that last year and
nothing happened." So the group effort comes to nothing.
To help to prevent this group suicide, use these typical
Negativist phrases as internal alarms to alert you to pay
attention to what's happening. Think: "Ah-hah! A Negativist at work! Watch the old depression there." Be alert
to your own irritation at all those "others" on whom your
life depends. This level of awareness should preclude *your*
getting drawn in. To help bolster your own defenses and
help others avoid being drowned in negativism, move on
to the next step.

State Your Own Realistic Optimism.

Poor conditions cannot always be alleviated. The forces
that maintain them may truthfully be overwhelming. Yet

there are always choices, alternative ways of moving with or against the stream. As I have watched groups and individuals deal with problems, I have become convinced that a serious and resourceful attempt at problem solving is invariably worthwhile. Even if the payoff is only in clarification, self-worth, and enthusiasm, it is enough.

Therefore, come back at negativism with an expression of your own realistic optimism. Be ready to say it twice if necessary. Here's what the dialogue might sound like:

YOU: We've got to pick up that package before to-morrow.

NEG: It's 5:10. They're closed.

YOU: Maybe someone will still be there.

NEG: Never. Those guys leave by 5:01 at the latest.

YOU: Sure, but remember last year when we knocked on the side door at the post office to get that Special Delivery letter. It was Sunday, and it took us fifteen minutes before anyone came, but the gal who answered the door got the letter for us.

If you don't have such a convenient example of a past success against the odds at hand, use an analogy from the past or an incident from home. If you can't think of anything concrete, a statement such as "I still have faith that we haven't tried everything" is better than nothing. Even this may help shore up your own commitment, and it may tip the internal balance in the others in favor of optimism—realistic, active optimism, of course, not a pie-in-the-sky, passive, hoping-for-the-best attitude.

Don't Argue.

You should not try to persuade Negativists to admit that they are wrong. First of all, they may not be. Satisfaction that you've done everything possible may be the only actual result from your problem-solving attempts.

Second, it's wasteful. Since they are starting with the certainty that nothing will work, they are not easily persuaded otherwise. The discussion can easily degenerate into a "You're wrong, I'm right" argument. If this happens, your efforts to wring that "I agree" from a Negativist will swamp whatever positive effect was achieved by your optimistic statements. After all, you don't know things will turn out well, but he or she does *know* they won't.

In the argument, it's clear who will sound most convincing. Instead of confronting the Negativist directly, your strategy should be one of showing that some alternatives are worth trying even if the Negativist *may* be right that they won't work.

Don't Rush into Proposing Solutions.

For as long as you can, avoid proposing solutions to whatever problem is under consideration. This advice is based in part on what is known about efficient problem-solving technique. The tendency to reach too quickly for answers, without waiting to complete the not-very-exciting step of clearly explicating the question, is pervasive. After all, why analyze when the solutions stare you in the face? This "steel trap mind" approach often does succeed. It produces fast answers that often work—when you're lucky and when the problem is truly simple. But it produces a lot of extra work if you're unlucky or the problem is complex.

When coping with a Negativist, two additional reasons suggest that the urge to "get moving" be restrained. First, the more that an issue is specified, by asking what, where, why, and how questions, the more clearly it exists as a problem, rather than simply as a complaint. My observation has been that active specification is seductively confounding to Negativists. As long as no one proposes solutions to be shot down, Negativists are free to get intrigued by the task of untangling a complex problem. For whatever reason, Negativists tend to move out of the limelight when the focus is on describing the problem, rather than passing judgment on it. (Oh, you've noticed that Negativists manage to be the center of attention without having to do anything at all?) The second additional reason for not rushing to solutions is that if you prematurely propose a possible way out of the problem, the Negativist will likely do well what he or she does best—explain why it won't work. As an extra bonus, you, and everyone else involved, are likely to get another dose of depression.

Set a Horror Floor.

When alternative actions are finally being generated, you can take *some* of the wind out of the Negativist's sails by asking what the worst consequences might be if a likely plan were implemented. "Look, just suppose that we were able to land this new landscaping contract with the bank. Yes, Rich, I understand that you don't think we could handle it, but if we did get it, what would be the worst things that could happen?" The process of looking straight down into the pit helps to differentiate real danger from plausible fantasy. It allows you to set the context for how negative views are to be interpreted and eases the minds of Negativists and others who might be immobilized by anxiety about potential "disasters."

Use Negativism Constructively.

Drags though they are, Negativists have a perspective that can be productively utilized in contingency planning. First, their focus on constraining forces can act as a needed counterweight to the over-optimism of others.

Second, when in your own mind you have separated the tone of helplessness and hopelessness from the *substance* of the negative comments, you may find them worth heeding. Recognizing that you don't have to explain them away, you can listen to them as useful cautions, aspects of the situation that need careful attention. Maybe the big boss *will* get sore when you send your memo. If you have anticipated this possibility, you can be sure that you *deliver* the memo. Then, if he sounds irked and defensive, you can move into a fall-back position, hastening to clarify that your intention was to aid the program, not to be destructive. In this way, you incorporate the Negativist's nose for gloomy prospects into a larger framework in which both negative and positive possibilities are given their proper credence.

Be Prepared to Go It Alone.

Be prepared to take appropriate action by yourself, even if the group remains under the Negativist's spell. Say to the Negativist, "Look, Don, I can see that you don't believe there is any hope for success in our sending this memo. I may be a complete fool, but I'm not convinced that, if carefully done, it won't work. I'm willing to take it on myself to get the data and write the memo. Now, if anyone else wants to be party to it, I can use all the help I can get. But, if not, I'll do it alone." Yes, there are costs. Striking out on your own does break the cohesiveness of the group. You are asserting your right not to be bound by a passivity you don't feel. You may even risk the Negativist going underground and sabotaging your effort, although I believe this to be a minimal danger. More likely, the Negativist, having had the reality of no hope acknowledged, may give you a helpful, if skeptical, assist in getting data on client complaints for your memo. By taking the initiative, you show an active, informed optimism that might spread to the other members of your group, even perhaps to the Negativist. But don't hold your breath.

Beware of Creating Negativism.

Although we have been considering how you can cope with Negativists, it's also well to observe how some actions can create negativism in individuals in whom it doesn't usually exist. Find one of those efficient people who are cautious and highly analytical and who like to understand fully what they're doing. Involve this person in a new undertaking and present it like this: "Here's the outline, Len. I want you to call all the district managers and go over this plan with them. Yes, there are good reasons for doing this; they're all included in these eight pages of back-up data. You can get into that tomorrow, but we need to start making phone calls this morning. I'll explain it all to you later."

At this point, Len will go back to his desk and do nothing for twenty minutes. Then he will come back behaving like a Negativist. He will say, "No, we can't do it" and "That'll never work." He will be resistant, he won't do anything well, and, in addition, he will be very upset by the process.

Those people who are fortunate enough to have methodical minds react very poorly when circumstances force them to take action when they have not yet fully understood what's going on. You will accomplish much more if you provide them with as much background information as you have, preferably a few days in advance. You, if you happen to have a different style of thinking, might in truth *not* look it over. People with methodical minds, however, will read it carefully and only then be ready to move. If time will not allow for their adequate preparation, I suggest you leave your high-powered analysts out of the rush-rush part of the job. Otherwise, be prepared for the unwelcome product of this very effective "Make-a-Negativist" kit.

REVIEW OF COPING WITH NEGATIVISTS

—Be alert to the potential, in yourself and in others in your group, for being dragged down into despair.
—Make optimistic but realistic statements about past successes in solving similar problems.
—Don't try to argue Negativists out of their pessimism.
—Do not offer solution-alternatives yourself until the problem has been thoroughly discussed.
—When an alternative solution is being seriously considered, quickly raise the question yourself of negative events that might occur if the alternative were implemented.
—See the doomsayings of the Negativist in perspective as potential problems to be overcome.
—At length, be ready to take action on your own. Announce your plans to do this without equivocation.
—Beware of eliciting negativistic responses from highly analytical people by asking them to act before they feel ready.

Chapter 7

BULLDOZERS AND BALLOONS: THE KNOW-IT-ALL EXPERTS

"You're really lucky, Paul, to have a chance to assist Dante Alfetto with that new series he's working on. He's one of the best directors in the business," Jack said, as he sat with his friend in a motion picture studio lunchroom.

"Yeah, I guess that's right," Paul said bitterly— "about him being the best director—but I don't think

I'm getting much out of it except the strong feeling that I'm an idiot. That guy is certain that he knows everything there is to know about making movies. He has a detailed plan for every scene worked out with diagrams, all done by numbers."

"Well, what's the problem with that? It's probably what makes him good."

"Sure," Paul replied, "but it leaves me with absolutely nothing to do except fetch and carry. My title is Assistant Director; it ought to be Chief Nothing. If I suggest something, he'll explain with that superior tone he's got just why it won't work. A month ago I gave him some script revisions. A week later I got them back covered with all kinds of snotty notes—'editorial corrections' he called them. Frankly, for the last two weeks I've just been sitting back and watching. What the hell, if he's so damned wonderful, he can do it himself."

"Now, have I made it quite clear why we should not put in a line of video-tapes?" Ames asked. "The volume of business we can expect and the cost of the tapes mean that we can't make a worthwhile profit from either selling or renting. I've looked into the matter thoroughly —the prices tapes are going for, the number of video-tapedecks there are around, all the market trends—and there's no question that I'm correct."

"Well, maybe you're right," Ted offered, "but I bet I could make it work."

"All right, that's enough," Ames cut in coldly. "I can't waste any more time on this. My father said you knew something about this business, but this video-tape idea certainly doesn't show it."

As he listened sullenly to young Phillip Ames, who had recently inherited the stereo and record shop he managed, Ted Wilson consoled himself. Next month, when that new nationally franchised stereo shop opened and started pushing video-tapes, Mr. Know-It-All Ames would lose his shirt.

Know-It-Alls like Dante Alfetto and Phillip Ames seem to occur everywhere in the work world. They convey a belief in their own superiority that often leaves us imperfect earthlings feeling humiliated, immobilized, and helplessly angry. Know-It-Alls come in two main variations, Bulldozers and Balloons. Both communicate with others as if they know everything there is to know. The difference is that Bulldozers do, indeed, know a great deal, while Balloons don't. In this chapter, we'll consider how to cope with each type.

BULLDOZERS

Let's listen in on Sid, a personnel technician, complaining about his boss, Virginia Dorne:

> There is just one way to do things around here: her way. You do it on her time schedule, you do it *only* in the manner she would do it, and you'd better know what that is. She doesn't want suggestions or to hear what you have to say. Just don't upset her with facts or with questions about whether the plan will work. It doesn't matter how much experience you've had with that kind of payroll system or that you *know* some of her ideas won't fly. All she seems to want you to do is shut up and pay attention. But if anything does go wrong, you can bet that it's you who weren't listening properly. Or else she goes slamming into her office and won't speak to anyone until she's worked out some elaborate explanation of what happened. Actually, 80 percent of her ideas are good ones, and I've learned a lot. But when she is wrong, it's a lulu. Setting things straight afterward sometimes takes months.

THE BEHAVIOR

Virginia Dorne, like Dante Alfetto, typifies the essential qualities of those very tough customers, the bulldozing, Know-It-All Experts. Bulldozers, as that name implies, are highly productive people, thorough and accurate thinkers who make competent, careful plans and then carry them through, even when the obstacles are great. They exude a feeling of power and personal authority and a self-sustaining quality that bespeaks the fact that they need others very little, if at all.

If these individuals are such gems of productivity, why are they included in a book on Difficult People? If you have ever found yourself teamed up with a Bulldozer as co-worker, supervisor, or subordinate, you know the answer. Here are the reasons I've come across most frequently.

(1) There is a tone of absolute certainty, of sureness

beyond mortal doubt, that, often without conscious intent, leaves others feeling like objects of condescension.

(2) Most frustrating of all is that these insufferable paragons of logic usually turn out to be absolutely right. Thus, they often leave others feeling inept, confused, or stupid.

(3) Bulldozers not only make their associates feel resentful, they also often elicit resistant, self-defeating behavior from them. For example, a group of engineers, as an act of protest, took to sending their reports to their bulldozing supervisor written carelessly in longhand on yellow-ruled note pads. "Why should we try to do good work," they explained. "Every report that goes up, no matter how carefully prepared, comes back covered with notes that tell us how lousy it is. So we rewrite it and it comes back again, sometimes four times. We got tired of the secretaries yelling at us because they had to retype the reports so many times."

(4) Bulldozers leave little room for anyone else's judgments, creativity, or resourcefulness.

(5) Once they set out to implement a plan of action, they are devilishly hard to dissuade, even when their plan appears to others to be headed for failure. Therefore, while Bulldozers are indeed usually correct, when they're wrong, it's often a disaster for everyone concerned.

(6) Finally, when things go wrong, they often see the fault as lying with those incompetents (like you and me) who were responsible for carrying it out.

Not all experts are Know-It-Alls. Experts are people who know a great deal about a particular topic and can use that knowledge to solve practical problems. They are often people of impressive humility. I have known a few whose competence was almost overlooked because they refused credit for successful group projects that were mostly theirs in conception and realization. The difference between plain, nondifficult experts and Bulldozers lies in the way they communicate their knowledge.

Since Bulldozers feel oracular, they see little need to listen to anyone else's facts or knowledge. They, you see, already know the best way to proceed. Thus, they respond with irritation, outright anger, or withdrawal to differing opinions, seeing them as personal contradictions rather than simply other interpretations of fact. When questioned about their ideas or plans, Bulldozers dump a profusion of detailed facts and elementary logical arguments on their questioners, leaving them feeling completely deluged or impatient. Worse, the data are often only marginally pertinent to the questions that were raised. In order to cope effectively with this avalanche, and the Bulldozer's superior attitude in general, we need to look more closely at what makes members of this species behave as they do.

UNDERSTANDING BULLDOZERS

Can you recall the way your parents sounded when they were telling you what you didn't know? "Put that knife down! Do you want to cut yourself?" "If you'll hold the bat off your shoulder a little more, Sonny, you'll get a better swing—thata boy!" "You'd better wear your raincoat, it looks like rain." Nothing differentiates children from their parents more than their unequal knowledge about the practical aspects of getting along in life. Parents don't simply think they have superior knowledge, they do, in fact, know more about what is safe, about what is likely to pay off and what is not, about almost anything their four-year-old kid is likely to encounter. Even the child's feelings are often more understandable to parents than to the child who has them.

For some children that parental aura of certainty about what is, and what's to come, represents security in a world that often feels unfathomable and inconsistent. For these children, the motivation to acquire facts and to develop orderly frameworks in which to fit those facts is particularly strong. The lesson for them is: Know for sure what the facts are; know for sure how they fit together—then, and only then, can you feel secure.

It is in this way that people are inclined, sometimes driven, to become experts, and what a constructive response to a wish for security it is. The problem for all would-be experts is that much of the world is very hard to nail down. "Facts" are perceived differently by different people. Opinions about what those facts mean vary even more. In the face of this pervasive ambiguity, some of us abandon any efforts to systematize our perceptions and simply respond to whatever turns up next. Others haven't abandoned these efforts, but have learned to live

with or even enjoy ambiguity and the seeming tentative-
ness of all knowledge. Still others, those Difficult People
we are trying to understand here, just can't stand such
uncertainty and strive even harder to impose their own
order on everything they can. Their certainty that their
theories, facts, and procedures *are* correct makes sane a
world otherwise too unpredictable to contemplate.

The basis of a Bulldozer's stability is that tightly held
knowledge which, given a changing world, constitutes the
only bedrock available. It is therefore not surprising that
an attack on the accuracy of that knowledge bites deep.
It strikes not only at the substantive matter under discussion, but also at deepest levels of personal motivation.
Thus, when the plan goes awry, the first line of defense
is the ineptitude of others. When that line does not hold,
and the cracks in that wall of logic must be faced, the
emotional impact can be catastrophic.

Complainers and Negativists, as we saw in preceding
chapters, feel that the forces that affect their lives are
largely out of their control. Bulldozers are the opposite.
Their early life experiences led to their construction of a
world in which they always got what they deserved.
Unequivocal praise or blame from parents plus a sense
of their own ability to affect things by careful planning
and follow-through led easily to the belief that if good
or bad things happen, they, not fate or luck, are the
cause.*

Given such strong needs to feel sure of their own no-
tions of reality and to depend upon their own efforts,
small wonder that Bulldozers spurn the ideas and conclusions of others. And each time the Bulldozer chugs
firmly and methodically to a planned objective, the security that comes from being self-directing, self-sustaining,
and unneedful of others is reinforced.

BULLDOZERS IN REVIEW

—Bulldozers have in common with nondifficult experts a
strong sense that the accumulation and ordering of facts

* No one fully understands the reasons that place a person at
one end or the other of the "who has control over my life" con-
tinuum. Perhaps it hinges more on chance outcomes to a few
crucial incidents rather than systematic parent-child relationships.
That these differences in where we place the locus of causality
do exist seems reasonably well demonstrated.

and knowledge can provide stability in a relatively whimsical world.
—Because Bulldozers believe that most of the power to affect their own lives resides in them, they tend to see the ideas and formulations of others as irrelevant to their own purposes.
—The "know-it-all" quality that seemed appropriate and equated with strength in their parents has become associated with both superiority and certainty of knowledge.

COPING WITH BULLDOZERS

The central strategy in coping with Bulldozers is to get them to consider alternative views while carefully avoiding direct challenges to their expertise, lest they take your recommendations as personal attacks on *them*. Four basic steps are involved: make adequate preparations; listen and acknowledge; question and suggest, don't challenge; and monitor your own tendencies toward bulldozing.

Do Your Homework.

The cardinal rule in effective coping with Bulldozers, or any experts for that matter, is that you *must, must* do your own homework. At the least this means you must marshal the facts that you need, be prepared with adequate backup materials, and be able to display your facts or proposal in an orderly way. It is particularly important that you make certain that all figures are accurate and calculations correct. You may be one who does that as a matter of habit, because there is a dash of expert in you, and you use it well. But if you are the type of person who is content, when coming up with the first draft of a proposal, to work out a "ball park" cost estimate without the benefit of a double check, I assure you, based on my own often painful experiences in coping with experts, that this will be the start of your downfall. It will likely be the end of it, too, since most experts, as a matter of course, will work over any figures or calculations to make sure they are correct. In the old pre-calculator days, out would come a ubiquitous yellow pencil and, without any interruption of the conversation, numbers would be crunched. Now, with the advent of pocket calculators, even complex calculations can be rapidly processed. One thing you can be sure of: if your numbers do not agree with what shows up on the register when your expert pushes the "equals" button that last time, you will have lost whatever potential influence you might have had. Experts will not take you seriously as a competent person worthy of trust if you seem to them unprepared or inaccurate. They won't even argue with you; they'll simply dismiss you as incompetent.

Listen and Acknowledge.

Experts usually doubt that their great wisdom has made its way into your poor weak mind. The best way to let them know that you comprehend what they say is to listen attentively to them. Try not to interrupt or cut them short. Then, paraphrase back to them the main points of their plan or the argument that they've been pursuing.

While listening and acknowledging does take valuable time at the beginning, it may save both time and tedium later. For one thing, it completes the communication cycle—always a valuable thing to do, because it insures that you are really receiving the meanings, not just the words that were sent. Since Bulldozers *usually* know what they're talking about, you may even learn something.

Another not insignificant benefit from active attention is that it may convey to Bulldozers that you appreciate and respect their importance and wisdom. This, in itself, is likely to diminish the Know-It-All quality of their communication.

The most important gain from paraphrasing is that it defends you against a flood of expert verbiage. When Bulldozers are not *sure* that you have fully understood the complexities of their plan, they tend to interpret questions or even a hesitation in agreeing with them as indications that you did not completely understand. After all, why else wouldn't you be in complete accord? You will then be treated to a repetition of the entire proposal, this time in great detail. As a chemical engineer client put it in speaking of one of his colleagues:

> I've learned never to ask any questions of Gordon. It actually saves me time to search through the chrono file instead and bring myself up to date on his work. If you even comment to Gordon, he seems to think

that you were asleep when he was talking. Then, here he comes with a detailed, chronological background statement on exactly how he came to his conclusions. And you can't stop him. He will run through everything, including formulas I learned in Physics IA. We've both been assigned to the same project team for next year, and how I dread it.

By paraphrasing you demonstrate to the Know-It-All that you do understand what he or she has said.

Question Firmly—but Don't Confront.

Whether you are a collaborator, a supervisor, or even a subordinate of a Bulldozer, the realities of life dictate that you will often have to point out something wrong or missing. Perhaps it will only be bringing up an issue that in your opinion was not adequately covered. Expect anyone with a streak of Bulldozer to take *personally* any statement that suggests a picture of reality different from his or her own.

For this reason, it is usually wise to use a questioning form to bring up issues or errors rather than the authoritative statement form that one might use with less touchy people. For example, you might say, "I'm have a little difficulty seeing how raising our prices will improve our market position. Will you explain that to me?" You do this even if your thought is: "All right, genius, how come you don't see that if we follow your plan, we'll price ourselves out of the market?" And even "We'll be overpriced for our competition" might be perfectly acceptable with a non-Bulldozer.

Although you shouldn't challenge your Bulldozer directly, do your best to raise your questions fully, firmly, and without equivocation. If your queries are too sketchy, they may be interpreted by the Bulldozer as proof of your ignorance. If they sound ingenuous or wheedling, they may be peremptorily dismissed—not exactly good for your relationship with the Bulldozer, or your ego.

By using a question format you present problems as new information to be considered and not as an attack on the Bulldozer's competence. Remember that Bulldozers are more deeply disturbed than most of us when faced with information that indicates that their map of the world is not as accurate as they thought it was and need it to be. If their knowledge base is challenged, they may do more of just what it was that you didn't want them to do in the first place—deny vehemently the possibility that there might be fruitful versions of reality other than their own.

Two techniques I've found most useful in capturing Bulldozers' interest in considering alternatives are to present the alternative as a detour and to ask what are called "extensional questions." These techniques work because they give you a chance to structure a conversation in a non-challenging way.

Present alternatives as detours. One of my partners has a knack for getting people with closed minds to pay attention to an alternative approach. He precedes his point with this: "I realize that this probably won't be what we'll end up with, but could we take a few minutes just to see if there might be anything useful there at all?" You would have to be a super Bulldozer to resist that.

Ask extensional questions. One of the most effective coping techniques is asking extensional questions. Extensional questions ask that a plan or a concept be mentally extended over time or space. "How will that concept look in practice?" and "Can you tell me how you envisage that program operating a year from now?" are examples. Basically, the purpose of extensional questions is to assist in moving the discussion from the conceptual to the concrete. The conversation sounds something like this:

> YOU: Frank. you seem to think that I *do* understand basically how your new accounting system will work. [He should; you just finished paraphrasing his ideas back to him, right?] Now, would you go through the steps that we'll take in implementing the system and describe what exactly will happen over the next six months?
>
> FRANK: Fine. The first thing we'll do is hire Innosys Computer Systems to develop the programs we'll need. Then we'll have to start transferring all the data from our old paper files onto tape and then . . . Hey—wait a minute—I just realized something. We're going to have to put on two additional accounting techs for that first year. Better get that change into the budget.

Perhaps you had already seen the need for a larger budget or perhaps you had not. The important point is that now Frank does. The new system will not start out crippled by a skimpy staff or with a budget overrun.

Pompous and dogmatic or not, Bulldozers are knowledgeable and competent in carrying out their own tasks. More than most, they are willing to look at, and be convinced by, facts and logic, *especially if it is their own facts and logic.* Your task is to help them avoid the terrible process that has sent many organizations led by Bulldozers to the bottom (incidentally, I believe the captain of the *Titanic was* such a person). Perhaps you have even seen this process at work: Bulldozers assemble facts, order them, and develop a prescriptive plan in which everything ought to work. They then proceed to spray it with liquid concrete. New facts? Dissonant data? They are either vehemently rejected or distorted with analytical embellishments to make them fit the plan. By asking extensional questions you force your Bulldozers to take a second look at their reality maps. But you do so constructively, in a climate that does not require that they be defensive to anyone but themselves.

Avoid Being a Counter-Expert.

To persons who see themselves as equally qualified, the overweening condescension of Bulldozers can be particularly intolerable. Without awareness of the intense interaction that may develop, even nondifficult people can lock themselves into a futile, sometimes catastrophic, struggle. Consider this example:

Clyde and Faye were principal members of a high-powered interdisciplinary scientific research group. From the beginning, there were seemingly endless wranglings among the members about how to set up a planning process. Then the meetings deteriorated into angry, stubborn bickerings, chiefly over proper procedures to be followed in documenting the results of the work to be done. No matter what Clyde would propose, Faye, with condescending patience, would refute it. Clyde felt caught in an interplay that disgusted him, but he could not seem to extricate himself from it. He turned to others in the group for support, for a way out. During the first few weeks, Trudy, the chairperson, seeing the problem, had tried several times to suggest a compromise. Faye would then argue with Trudy. Clyde would restate his original plan, and the cycle would begin again, leaving Clyde ready to quit and the group demoralized.

Everyone, it seemed, knew that Faye, top biologist that she was, was also a pain. But Clyde was known as a usually level-headed person, able to calmly carry through with his ideas. What had happened, as I learned in a subsequent private conversation with Clyde, was that he had felt his own expertise challenged by Faye. Six months previously his very well received book entitled *Planning for the R and D Administrator* had come out. With good cause, he had considered himself an authority on research planning, and he keenly resented Faye. Her challenge to his own sense of competence had caused him to pull his own rusty steamroller into action. In such battles, Bulldozers usually win, however. Their motivations are usually stronger. Their many successes in pushing through their own point of view have given them a persistence that occasional headknockers such as Clyde have not developed.

If you should find yourself in Clyde's position, your own sense of being an expert aroused, here are some actions that may help.

Listen to yourself. Be alert to a patronizing sound in your own voice, stubborn digging in, or a wish to withdraw into irritated boredom. These are indications that the interaction is bringing out the worst in you.

Acknowledge the Bulldozer's competence. Saying "I respect your viewpoint because I consider you an expert in this field" never hurt anyone's ability to be heard by a Bulldozer. Be ready, however, to have your statement disregarded. Your Bulldozer may consider your opinion inconsequential. Because this acknowledgment particularly helps when your Bulldozer has a tinge of hostile aggressiveness, I believe it worthwhile; the move can't hurt and may help.

Make time for reflection. It is frequently useful to respond to a Bulldozer's pronouncements with something like the following: "Look, Faye, from our discussion I think I see what you're after. It's well thought out and may *be* the way to go, but right now I still can't buy all of it. Let me think it over for a while." This can be followed by: "Can I ask this. Take my ideas under consideration—maybe you can work them into something."

This pause accomplishes two things. First, it gives the Bulldozer an opportunity to consider what you've suggested. All experts are better influenced when they have sufficient time to absorb thoroughly any new sets of data. They will, in fact, reject proposals out of hand if they feel incompetent because everyone else seems to know what's going on. Second, a break in the interaction gives you time to regroup and remind yourself that the objective is to get something done, not wipe that demeaning sneer off your Know-It-All's face. Thus, at the next meeting you will be set to ask extensional questions, be firmly tentative, or at least be able to carry off the next coping step.

A Last Resort: Let Them Be the Experts.

What if none of these steps seem to work? Your Know-It-All continues to insist on his or her own view of reality, acting patronizing or condescending about your plans, taking credit for all successes while denying or rationalizing away problems that arise. Is there anything to do other than get out, and hang the cost?

There is yet one possibility that can create a relatively static-free relationship, even with possibilities for improvement. It has, however, a sizeable psychological cost. The cost is that you have to swallow your pride and *purposefully* act deferentially to these "superior" beings, even when they are your organizational equals or subordinates. You will listen attentively, blink your eyes, and, with careful diligence, dance to their tunes. In effect, you will be saying to them, "All right, you great big wonderful, all-knowing fountains of wisdom, give me advice, lay out the plans, tell me what you're going to do; and I'll help you do it." By taking this subordinate stance your interactions should become reasonably free from static and generally more comfortable. An obvious gain is that, within the limits of the competence of your Bulldozer, you can work productively. More to the point, if you can carry it off, you should feel less tension and anger.

The behavior that I am talking about here is indeed *coping* behavior. It is far different from an unaware and unplanned reaction to a superior tone and maddening certitude. That kind of unconscious resistance shows up as sabotage, backbiting, or in your own creeping ineptness. Even worse, it can twist into anger directed against yourself, leaving you feeling depressed or angrily hopeless.

Coping behavior, chosen with a full awareness of just what you're doing and why, is quite different. After all, you have *not* been able to find a way to relate constructively to this person. Why should that condemn you to a state of internal uproar? By consciously *choosing* to cope in this way, you maintain your self-integrity. You also prevent the growth of that deeper tension that occurs when you let yourself *reactively* behave in a way inconsistent with your own values. By making a practical decision to cope, you remain the one in control of your own behavior.

Choosing this move of last resort does not preclude your using every other coping step you can find, including those mentioned here. This additional effort is worth making for this rather surprising reason: because of your competent assistantship, that Bulldozer may begin to see you in a new light, as an expert in your own right. After all, haven't you recognized and been supportive of the truth at its very source? Haven't you seen what a wise and wonderful person he or she is? The next you know, your Bulldozer may be talking with you about the difficulties of getting the message across to all those other pigmies out there, the ones you *both* have to endure. Since Bulldozers are often people of authority and weight, this "equal" (well, almost equal) relationship can be most valuable.

To those of you who may be feeling resistant to the idea of making such tender efforts with Bulldozers, I point to your alternatives: (1) Sit there wishing they were different and steam; (2) Sabotage any plan you can and possibly sink the ship (and you along with it); (3) Throw a tizzy and prove that they were right all along; (4) Get out; or (5) Effectively cope.

REVIEW OF COPING WITH BULLDOZERS

—Make sure you have done a thorough job of preparing yourself; carefully review all pertinent materials and check them for accuracy.

—Listen carefully and paraphrase back the main points

of the Bulldozer's proposals, thus avoiding over-explanation.

—Avoid dogmatic statements.

—To disagree be tentative, yet don't equivocate; use the questioning form to raise problems.

—Ask extensional questions to assist in the re-examination of plans.

—Watch your own bulldozing tendencies by:

listening for Know-It-All behavior in yourself.

conveying your appreciation of the Bulldozer's knowledge.

proposing delays in action to gain time for each to review the ohter's proposals.

—As a last resort, choose to subordinate yourself to avoid static and perhaps to build a relationship of equality in the future.

BALLOONS: THOSE PHONY KNOW-IT-ALL EXPERTS

My husband, Carl, has a habit of sounding off on anything, whether he knows what he's talking about or not. I have to admit that he's very good with words. Most of what he says sounds plausible to anyone who knows less than he does. For example, the other day he insisted that the cause of our neighbor's car trouble was a cracked wheel bearing. He was so convincing that Steve, the neighbor, refused to let a garage mechanic, who said it was something else, work on the car. It ended up costing him $250 extra for labor by the time he finally got it fixed. I wanted Carl to apologize to Steve, but my husband couldn't understand why I thought he owed Steve anything. "Steve's a grown-up man," he said. "He makes his own decisions."

THE BEHAVIOR

Carl, the auto expert (and, incidentally, a university professor of English), is a phony Know-It-All expert. To describe these annoying and sometimes troublesome people, the term *Balloon*—"an object with thin flexible walls filled with hot air or gas"—seems apt. Balloons speak with great authority about subjects of which they have little knowledge, and even that little knowledge may be inaccurate. They read newspaper articles and become instant experts, propounding on the subjects sketchily described in the articles without mentioning the source of their great store of knowledge. Balloons range in scope from inept braggarts, easily seen through, to pompous and imperious tyrants like Phillip Ames, whom we met at the beginning of the chapter, to articulate and skillful "experts" like Carl, who spread bewilderment wherever they go. Because some Balloons are so smoothly convincing, it can be difficult to differentiate them from Bulldozers. Often the only way you can be sure you are faced with a *phony* expert is to be a genuine expert yourself, knowing what the facts are and how they should properly be put together.

Balloons are not simply liars or con-artists. What distinguishes liars and con-artists from Balloons is that liars and con-artists always know that they're being deceptive, and they have a purpose clearly in mind, usually involving gain for them. Balloons, by contrast, at the moment of truth (or, should we say, untruth) believe that they know what they're talking about.

UNDERSTANDING THE BEHAVIOR

I have thought about what produces Balloons for a long time, probably because I suspect there is more than a little in me. At the heart of Balloon motivation seems to be the overwhelming desire to be admired and respected by others. Not so much to be liked as to be thought well of and seen as a person of importance. How better to get this approbation than by confidently showing how much you know about whatever is being discussed?

As a learned strategy this works even better if you are unknowingly deceptive. For those who want respect for their expertise, the bonding of reality and wish fulfillment will blur and *at the moment of speaking* they will feel sure that they are putting out the true word. Suppositions come to represent reality and speculation becomes a glowing gem of wisdom. This is the sequence of internal events, mostly out of the Balloon's focus of awareness, that reinforces the continued use of this defective thinking pattern. In schematic form, it goes like this:

(1) I want them to see how brilliant (knowledgeable, wonderful, competent) I am;

(2) What I'm thinking sounds so plausible, it's probably true;

(3) If it is true, why not say so;

(4) Well, nobody has called me a liar, so I guess it was true. Now I know I'm brilliant.

Balloons are often very curious people. Couple this with the fact that they like to feel "in the know" and you have the potential for a crazyquilt of knowledge about the world. They read newspapers, browse through the first four chapters of many books, listen hard to the rumor mill, and eavesdrop wherever they can. What a great way to acquire scraps and bits of knowledge about lots of interesting things. The problems start when they try to sell the popcorn they make from all of these kernels of fact.

BALLOONS IN REVIEW

—Balloons seek the admiration and respect of others by acting like experts when they are not.

—They often are only partially aware that they are speaking beyond their knowledge.

—Balloons are often curious and alert to information. This useful quality leads to trouble only when sketchy or abbreviated information is asserted as a full and accurate picture of the situation.

COPING WITH BALLOONS

Balloons, in comparison to other types of Difficult People we've met in this book, are usually minor league headaches. Once you are on to them, phony experts can even be likeable. You can, with deliciously patronizing fondness, let them pontificate about subjects they clearly know little about. Just pay them the attention they seek and feel benevolent about having done such a good deed.

When Balloons are not in positions of influence, most people feel only mild irritation, impatience, or embarrassment when forced to deal with them, not the anger and frustration attributed to other Difficult People. "Should I stop this character from misleading everyone?" is the usual internal question that arises.

When Balloons are influential people, however, their interweavings of reality with speculation and wish can lead to real trouble. They will propose a course of action based upon plausible but false assumptions which, given their authority or charisma, may just be acted on. The result: a confused waste of energy and the dilution of everybody's sense of purpose. A near disaster brought on by a Balloon in power was described to me by a new personnel director.

> I don't think anyone really knows how close to a huge fiasco we came last fall. Willis Schaefer, our former boss—a very competent technical personnel man, by the way—decided after hearing a lecture on the subject that we needed an employee counseling program. He proceeded, all by himself, to work up a presentation for top management. It was a silly, superficial plan that would have cost a fortune and gotten us into trouble with the union to boot. But he talked so knowingly to the big boys about it that even before the plan was formally presented, they were ready to buy it. Thank God he was hired away by another company and the whole scheme evaporated.
>
> Why didn't one of us blow the whistle? Two reasons, I'd say. First, when he came back from that lecture and talked about employee counseling we were all for it. The plant needed something along that line. Then, before we could do anything, he was telling very important people just how it ought to be done. It was *so* wrong that anything we could have said at that point would have made him out to be a fool.

There, elegantly laid out, is the basic Balloon coping problem. How do you make sure that the Balloon's unworkable idea will be quashed without making him or her out to be either a charlatan or a fool? After all, nothing is easier than devastating phony experts. A loud and clear "Baloney!" backed by accurate and documented facts, will penetrate the cover and expose them as imposters. Tempting as it is in fantasy, this is rather tough medicine, especially if you need to work or live with these folks. Here's an equally effective and much kinder approach. It has the added advantage that, if you happen to be mistaken and your Balloon turns out to be a Bulldozer, you will not get mashed.

State the Facts as an Alternative Version.

As in the direct kill approach, the first step in coping with Balloons is to give a descriptive statement of the facts, as you believe them to be. But instead of yelling "Baloney" (or its earthy equivalent), present your data as an alternative set of facts rather than the only set.

Give the Balloon a Way Out.

Provide your Balloon a face-saving vehicle, because at the moment of truth (here meant literally) he or she will be immobilized. The presence of a real expert suddenly brings to full awareness the shakiness of the ground on which the phony has been walking. The probability of a disastrous loss of face, on the other hand, will reduce the Balloon to the most elemental kind of defensive behavior.

Let's see how these simple steps would have worked with Carl:

CARL: There's no question about it, Steve, that rattle in your Cyclone's rear end is a bearing. It couldn't be anything else. Don't let those guys try to sell you an axle replacement job. Cyclone axles last forever. I've never heard of one having to be replaced.

STEVE: Well, the guy at the garage said he thought something might have gone wrong with the axle housing and it was maybe eating into the . . .

YOU (an expert on Cyclones): You know, Carl, that fits with some things that I've been reading about Cyclone axle problems. It's possible that too great a strain on the frame, from pulling a trailer, say, can throw the axle housing out of line. I wonder if

It's easier for a bystander to cope with a Balloon. However, Steve could have done the same thing if he had been an expert on Cyclones.

you could be thinking about those Cyclone axles prior to 1972. I think the situation may have been different then.

CARL: Oh, yeah . . . maybe that's what I was thinking about.

YOU: I don't think that repair job will cost you more than $250, Steve.

It helps to be ready to fill in with some conversation. Gives the Balloon a chance to recover.

Alone Is Better.

My experience with Balloons is that facing them with the facts is more easily done without company. Helping anyone save face is far simpler when it's only your opinion that is at stake. You may wish, however, to come prepared with a handy suggestion about how the Balloon's public announcement of the state of the treasury (which you've just shown to be grossly incorrect) might be handled with a minimum of embarrassment. I know it's tempting to let them suffer, but . . .

REVIEW OF COPING WITH BALLOONS

—State correct facts or alternative opinions as descriptively as possible and as your own perceptions of reality.
—Provide a means for the Balloon to save face.
—Be ready to fill the conversation gap yourself.
—Cope with a Balloon when he or she is alone, when possible.

Chapter 8

INDECISIVE STALLERS

Janet was bright, inquisitive and full of ideas. When she was given account responsibility and moved into the New Products section she felt her star was at last rising. Initially, she had found Donna one of the most helpful and supportive supervisors she could recall in her thirteen years at work. Trouble started, however, when Janet's section was transferred to a new department. Donna, still her boss, now came under the direction of a newly appointed department head, whom we'll call Mr. Bennett because his subordinates never used his first name. Janet noticed a change in her supervisor immediately. She described it this way:

> Donna began to take longer and longer to make a decision. Before, she had given me a lot of latitude, but suddenly she needed to okay everything I did. For example, she wanted to approve, in advance, a series of marketing letters, even though they were very similar to ones that, on my own, I had sent out rather successfully three months before. It wasn't that she was resistant to my ideas. It was just the opposite: I could persuade her to support practically anything I wanted to do. What was so aggravating—and it took me a while to realize what was happening—was that she would continually change her mind; and then I would persuade her again and then she would change her mind again. I became aggressive, then impatient, fighting for what I felt was the right decision. At one point I even wrote a cover note for her to send upstairs with a memorandum of mine. I handed it to her with a pen, and waited right there while she signed it. She signed it all right, and then left it on my desk the next morning with a note telling me not to do anything further on the project.
>
> I went around her on two occasions, neither of them very successful. The second time brought hurt and tearful questions from her about my loyalty. Then I couldn't hold back my exasperations of the preceding months any longer. I let go with some cruel sarcasm and accused her of being weak. Donna turned and left the room without another word. The next day, we both tried to act as if nothing had happened, but things between us became worse and worse. We did our business at a distance. I would drop notes on her desk at lunchtime and she would send memos back to me through the interoffice mail. It kept things going, but the effect on my work—and my morale—was disastrous.

Mack was the technically competent owner and general manager of a large service company; Tom was his forceful and highly involved production manager; and Bob was an unproductive but likeable floor foreman. I was consulting with both Mack and Tom.

The problem surfaced first at a management meeting at which Bob had complained bitterly about not having been selected for promotion to the department head level. Mack pointed out that Bob had never made a formal application for the job, implying that he should do so the next time there was an opening.

The next day, at a meeting attended only by Tom, Mack, and me, Tom vented his frustration. Those who worked with Bob, he said, knew that he hadn't been worth much for at least three years. "Why then," he asked Mack, with only partially concealed irritation, "did you imply to Bob that you'd promote him if he'd only apply?" At this meeting, and in many subsequent conversations with him, Mack contritely acknowledged that he had a problem with Bob. He clearly saw the need to tell Bob straight out that he had not been promoted because he did not deserve promotion *and* that if he wished to be promoted, he needed to produce.

Four months later, Tom's feeling of frustration had turned to bewildered anger:

> When something pushes Mack the wrong way, he gets on me about increasing productivity and getting jobs out faster. But when I pass the message on down, the people on the floor resent it. I don't blame them, either. They all know that some people, Bob being the worst, are only carrying half a load because they knew the boss in the old days. I can't get on Bob myself—and I've tried a number of times—because he thinks I'm just being unfair and authoritarian. He can always go in and talk things over with "good old Mack." *You* know how many times Mack has decided that he ought to read the riot act to Bob. I've mentioned it four times myself in the last four months. Each time he agrees with me, sounds guilty, and makes excuses, but I know hell will freeze over before he actually does it.

THE BEHAVIOR

When you must depend on other people to do things for you—sending important letters, signing order forms or checks, assigning grades, taking your proposals to a higher level, or turning in their pieces of your project—

nothing is more maddening than to find out that those at
whose mercy you've been put can't make up their minds.
It is precisely your dependency on them that makes these
indecisive people so damnably frustrating: to be full of
enthusiasm and conviction yourself, only to be stone-
walled by them. To make it worse, often there seems to
be nothing to do and no way to fight.

Individuals who can't make up their minds are of many
types. Individuals like Donna and Mack, however, represent an especially difficult kind of indecisive person. I
call them Stallers because of their tendency to stall off
major decisions until they go away. Like others who can't
make up their minds, Stallers become problems only when
something in your own life depends on their taking action.
If it weren't for the fact that *you* need some action from
them, why, they could be as indecisive as they wish, and
blessings on them. But when you do need that decision
made or that report submitted, woe unto you.

Of course, everyone is, or ought to be, indecisive at
times. When you're faced with two alternatives, both of
which are equally attractive or awful, taking a little time
to think the situation through is wise. Even taking a great
deal of time is warranted, if the time is spent in study,
analysis, or self-searching, and if the consequences are
great. But Stallers do not simply prolong the decision-
making process, they avoid it, sometimes to absurd and
unproductive limits. Unproductive for you, because that
decision on which you depend isn't made, but unproductive for them as well, because they aren't moving
toward a solution, just sitting on the problem.

In their defense, it should be noted that Stallers are
almost always pleasant and supportive, especially when
they are sitting on your decision. That's precisely what
makes them so frustrating to do business with. They
usually listen well, nod their heads encouragingly, look
interested—and are—and ask pertinent, if unchallenging,
questions. You are likely to leave this interaction quite
sure that they have decided in your favor. When you
come back a week later, however, no action has been
taken. There has been a delay, perhaps a few second
thoughts, someone whose concurrence was needed just
happened to be unavailable. Two weeks later, still no
action. After three weeks, when and if you inquire about
the decision, your Staller expresses concern for you. He

or she listens sympathetically, though uncomfortably, apologizing for the delay, perhaps tentatively pointing out some complications in the situation, but never really saying yes or no. You discuss the few complications, get more positive response, but this time you leave confused. What's happening? Where did it slip? What can I do now? Most of those from whom we gathered data had given up by the time three months of indecision had elapsed. Many had tried to run around, or over, their Stallers. All but those who had learned to cope on their own felt, not suprisingly, frustrated, defeated, or angry.

What causes Stallers unwittingly to visit such unhappiness on others, and how can their equivocal behavior patterns be successfully circumvented?

UNDERSTANDING THE BEHAVIOR

Ironically, the stalling behavior that causes you anguish comes from people who are powerfully and genuinely motivated to be helpful to others. This strong desire to be helpful presents them with a terrible dilemma when they move into roles that require decisions. For any important decision has the potential for bringing disappointment or distress to someone. In organizational life, in the community, at school, and even at home, decisions always distribute valuable and scarce resources: money, time, high grades, attention, and caring. Thus, they are inevitably tied to people's wants and hopes. The terrible conflict faced by Stallers is this: "However I decide, someone will not like it. I cannot knowingly and directly hurt anyone. What am I to do?"

Their primary desire to be helpful is what differentiates Indecisive Stallers from another type of Difficult Person that we've already encountered, the Super-Agreeable. Both Indecisive Stallers and Super-Agreeables tell you things that are satisfying. Both are Difficult People precisely because they leave you believing they are in agreement with your plans, only to let you down. But the motivation is different. Super-Agreeables can't tell you no because they fear the loss of your approval. Stallers, by contrast, can't reach a decision because they can't bear to hurt anyone.

Associated with the motivation of Stallers to help others is a strong concern for doing things in a way that will contribute most to the general welfare. At the level of practical living, the altruistic person feels bound to do what is right and proper rather than what is expedient. In other words, it is quality rather than speed, efficiency, or quantity that counts. Stallers place such an emphasis on quality and value that they may sit on a plan that doesn't do everything for everybody, saying to themselves, "It won't do well enough by our clients"; "The quality control standards aren't high enough"; "Our staff won't like it." Never mind that we need a program *now*. Your plan isn't of high enough quality.

While high standards are greatly to be valued, there is also, at times, much to be said for rapid and responsive action, even if it's occasionally "quick and dirty." This type of action Stallers just cannot bring themselves to do.

If Stallers knowingly apply heroic standards to themselves and their projects, it's crucial to realize that they unconsciously apply the same standards to you. This makes them easily disappointed and angry, especially if you do not seem to care in the way they think you should. The result may be withdrawn commitment to you or to your project or plan, with, need I say, no direct message to you about what they are feeling.

Confronted with dilemmas, Stallers have devised a marvelous way out that, like the strategies of other Difficult People I've described, bring short-term benefits at higher long-run costs. The Staller's peculiar escape is simply to stall everyone long enough; thus the need for any decision disappears. The events of life have a wonderful way of moving on, rapidly erasing the need for *any* decision. Here are a few examples:

3:30 P.M.: "Can we go to the movies tonight, Mom?"
"Maybe. Wait 'til Daddy gets home."
6:00 P.M.: "Can we go, huh?"
"I don't know yet."
7:15 P.M.: "What, the movies? No, dear, it's too late to go."

May 15th: "Boss, I'd like to hire on some extra help to meet that marketing project deadline. Could you okay my using some of the salary savings that have accrued in the budget?"
"I'll ask the controller."

June 1:   "I could still use that extra help, Boss."
            "Well, there's evidently a delay in getting it
            approved—I'll see the controller again."
July 1:   "Sorry, but all the salary savings have re-
            verted back to the General Fund."

What an elegant system. Neither Mom nor Boss had to make anyone feel bad by saying, "No, we've overspent our entertainment budget," or "No, if you'd use the staff you have more efficiently you wouldn't need extra help." In these ways, the Staller avoids inflicting *direct* distress on anyone.

Elegant or not, attempting to lower internal pressure by procrastination exacts a great toll from all concerned. The costs of stalling are:

—Alternate ways of getting a job done are not considered.

—Those on the receiving end of the indecision lose enthusiasm and commitment.

—Despite their success at evading the decision, Stallers invariably feel high levels of tension as they experience conflicting demands on them. Remember, Stallers care about people.

To remain pleasant and supportive and at the same time evade decision making, most Stallers have become masters at indirect communication. How else can you function when your sense of the right and proper thing to do seems to dictate that you tell others distressing news? To handle this conflict, Stallers have learned to converse in a way tangential to the real issues. People on the receiving end of this indirection are left with a confused and anxious feeling, but no substance. What they ought to have heard was some candid feedback on their performance, or criticism of their plans. But they get instead a mixture of hints and vague allusions. Of course, it takes two to obfuscate. Most of us don't *like* to hear negative things, even when we believe it would be good for us to hear them. The temptation is great to let the hints go by rather than follow them up with a clarifying question. Thus, conversations transpire in which everything is said except what is really meant. This, for instance, is what happened when Mack finally "confronted" Bob with his poor performance:

"Well, Bob," Mack began, "the reason that I've asked you to come in is that, after talking about you with Dr. Bramson, I realized that I had, uh, never really told you about how much we appreciate all the things you've done around here."

Bob nearly fell out of his chair since Tom had told him that Mack was going to come down very hard. Tom looked appalled, while I sat there desperately trying to think of something to say to keep the meeting from becoming a fiasco. I finally mustered a "You look a little confused, Bob."

"Well," he started, "it's very nice to hear that from Mack but . . ."

Mack, getting into the swing of things, looked at Tom and said, "You know, we don't have any system for getting the word out to the troops about how they're doing. The annual appraisals are a farce. We ought to have a series of staff development meetings, with every guy in the plant." With a master's stroke, he then turned to me and asked, "What do you think, Dr. Bramson?"

I glanced at Tom, who, grasping at any straw, was nodding his head, and then at Bob. He was still confused, but glad to have become a bystander. Obviously no help there. With no idea of how to "help" Mack, I found myself allowing as how a planned development process was usually a good idea. That was all Mack needed. With a cheery, "Will you take care of it, Tom," he stood up and looked quizzically at Bob. Was there anything more Bob wanted, he wondered. There wasn't.

STALLERS IN REVIEW

—Stallers are super-helpful, indecisive people who postpone decisions that might distress someone.

—This "works," because as life proceeds, most decisions, if unmade, quickly become irrelevant.

—Stallers hint and beat around the bush as a compromise between being honest and not hurting anyone.

COPING WITH STALLERS

You might presume, as Tom did initially about Mack, that your Staller will eventually make that decision and get on with life. You can indeed *hope* that everyone will be direct and candid, and will *not* decide for others whether or not they can take being a little or a lot distressed. My experience, however, is you're in for trouble if you count on it. For that is just what *these* difficult, indecisive, indirect people cannot—and do not—do. Your choice, as usual, is clear: sit there and be frustrated and continue to wish that they were different, or recognize that Stallers are not going to be candid unless you make it as easy as possible for them.

Well, how can you cope with people so frustratingly helpful to yourself or others, to help them get off the dime and move, or at least be direct and honest about why they're not? Here are some methods that work much of the time.

Surface the Issues.

The indispensable first step in successful coping with Stallers is to find out the real reasons your nemesis is stalling. Only then can you do some productive problem solving, with them or for them. That, my friends, may be very difficult to do. There you are, enthusiastic, desperately wanting to have your project approved or your product purchased. Unfortunately, to the extent you communicate that enthusiasm and hope (and how can you help it?), you increase the Staller's inability to tell you directly about those little hang-ups that are standing in the way of approval. These actions can help you to surface the issues.

Make it easy for them to be direct. Stallers are afraid to make important decisions because they may hurt someone. You can help them be candid by letting them know that you won't be impossibly wounded by learning their possible reservations. Here is the kind of question that makes it as easy as possible for Stallers to be candid: "Even a good project (thesis, product, service) has some things about it not quite as good as the best. Could we talk about those? I'd welcome your comments on even small things that could use improvement." Keep in mind that those "small things" might be the tips of just the icebergs that are keeping the Staller from proceeding.

Remember, although you know that you can take honest criticism or any other kind of bad news, your Staller doesn't know.

Pursue signs of direction. You may get some clues as to

where to focus your attention by listening for language that seems indirect, evasive, or justifying. Here are some examples: "I think that this is a generally well worked-out report" (what does "generally" mean?). "There's no doubt in my mind that this is what should be done" (why not *will* be done?). "All in all, your report is coming along quite nicely" ("all in all"?).

Stallers experience a strong internal pressure to be honest. That is why they hint, imply, or use weasel words rather than telling outright lies. By gently asking them about the meaning of indirect words, omissions, or hesitations, you help them resolve their inner conflict by a slide into honesty. For example, my breakthrough with Mack came when he said, for the second time during a consulting session, "There is just no doubt that I should tell Bob all the things that I've been telling you." I raised my eyebrow and said, "Should?" He sat very still, staring at me. I explained that since he seemed convinced that honesty with Bob was the proper course, there must be some other good reason for his hesitation. He closed his eyes for a moment, sighed, and finally said: "You know, there is something that bothers me every time I think about sitting down with Bob. He has had some problems with his wife; she's ill now. I doubt that anyone here knows about all the trouble he's had through the years. I know it has nothing to do with what I ought to do, but every time I pick up the phone to ask him to come in, I think, 'What if he's just had a call from home?' And then, instead of dialing, I pull something else off my in-basket."

Here are some examples of Staller indirection and ways to follow up:

YOU: I'd like to handle this next sale myself.
STALLER: Yes, I think one person *could* handle this sale better than two.
YOU: Do I pick up that you think I'm not ready yet? Tell me more. I want to get on to this kind of selling as soon as I can.

YOU: I just can't make it at school on my current allowance.
STALLER: I guess kids just have to buy more things than when I was in school.

YOU: Could we talk about anything that I'm spending money on that seems unnecessary to you?

Sometimes Stallers aren't aware that they feel conflict over a decision. They feel worried, angry, depressed, or guilty, but the source of these feelings may elude them. It can't hurt, and often will help, to simply ask "What's the conflict?" when you sense that someone with a touch of Staller in them is immobilized.

Consider that it might be you. It is easy to underestimate the difficulty of surfacing the underlying obstacle to a decision. There is no end to the number of plausible reasons that can be given for anyone's inaction, and Stallers are adept at presenting them. These Difficult People easily lull you into optimistically waiting forever, or aggressively pushing on the wrong doors.

Discovering the stumbling block is especially difficult when the underlying issue is you. If your Staller doubts your ability, loyalty to the group (a common doubt of Stallers, by the way), or commitment to the task, he or she will tell everyone but you. Therefore, keep an eye on yourself. Negative feedback may build your character but it is rarely fun to hear. It is always a temptation to let a Staller's hints go by the board and not question neutral-sounding rationalizations, such as "The budget's been cut" or "I don't think we can take the time right now." Remember, Stallers are skillful at helping you *not* face hard realities.

Is there a possibility that trying to surface your Staller's reservations may worsen the situation? Having told you, "I've already promised the money to Sam," will your Staller then find it easy to say, "Therefore, you're out of luck," when he or she might have looked for money elsewhere? Yes, there may be times when helping a Staller spill the beans will tip the scales of a decision against you. But the alternative—continuing to try to persuade that indecisive person *without* bringing to light the nature of the doubts—seems to me to be the more dangerous.

When you have left, the indecisive person will be alone with his or her thoughts. He or she will feel guilt about those unexpressed doubts that were never fully stated or resolved, perhaps not even consciously experienced. Guilt seldom leads to positive and vigorous action, however. The likely result is more yes-no equivocation. On the positive side of trying to uncover the problem is the fact that Stallers are more than ready to help you over a hurdle once its existence has been acknowledged.

Help Them to Problem Solve.

Once the underlying issues are out in the open, you are in a position to help Stallers solve *their* problem with the decision. If they don't escape their bind, you don't get a decision. Your approach should be slightly different depending on whether or not you are the source of the reservation.

If it's you. When you finally get that admission, "Do you really think you have the experience to tackle this job?" you should do the following.

1) Acknowledge your weaknesses. Acknowledging past failures or deficiencies in skill or experience will gain trust, especially from Stallers. They are usually responsive to honest admissions of past problems and to requests for help, seeing these acknowledgments as signs of strength.

2) State facts nondefensively. If there are facts unknown to your Staller relevant to the decision, state them as descriptively as possible. "Did you know that government budget cuts have reduced the size of my grant for the last two years?" If you sound hurt or defensive, you will get sympathy and more unreal assurances—but no decision.

3) Propose a plan. Stallers are concerned with you and your feelings. That's nice but it gets in the way of their realizing that you might be willing to sacrifice something for a good cause (or, at least, a cause that's good for you). You can point out your willingness by proposing a resolution in which you don't gain immediately. "Suppose you fund Bill's project this year and put me first on the list for any money saved out of next year's salary and wages," you might suggest. "Meanwhile, I'll send in samples of my work so you can see the progress I'm making."

If it's not you. If you are not the cause of your Staller's indecision, you should move on to asking problem-solving questions. You can help almost anyone who is faced with a dilemma by asking him or her to describe the problem in as much revelant detail as possible. This helps pose issues clearly, the prelude to definitive decision making. When Mack, for instance, finally blurted out his sympathetic concern for Bob's family situation, he was able to move on. Bob's sick wife wasn't the "cause" of Mack's long procrastination as much as the Staller component in Mack's own personality. Bob's wife was, however, the situational element that evoked the stalling. These problem-solving questions helped Mack articulate the problem he was having: "Is there ever a time when Bob is less distressed by his home situation?" "What would be the least stressful way of bringing up the subject?" "Would it be helpful to have someone else sit in on the discussion?"

Mack discovered that there *were* times when Bob was relatively free from pressures in his home life. His wife, who suffered from a chronic but relatively mild mental illness, was occasionally hospitalized for several weeks at a time. During those periods Bob was, at least in Mack's perception, more relaxed, if not more productive. Mack decided to write down his perception of Bob's performance. He asked Bob into his office, gave him the confidential memo, and left him to read it. He then returned and made good use of his ability to listen. In the final step, Mack walked Bob down to Tom's office, where they discussed performance standards and promotions. I sat in, mostly to symbolize that it was now a new game. Also to keep Tom from saying, "I told you so."

Rank-Order Alternatives.

If you can, persuade the Staller to limit the number of alternatives to be considered. Stallers have enough trouble deciding between two. Five can be completely immobilizing. Limiting alternatives is sometimes hard to do because of that built-in problem of Stallers—they want to do everything for everybody.

An effective way to induce your Staller to limit alternatives is to propose that they be ranked by desirability. Stallers will be more likely to go along with a prioritizing approach than a simple, yes, we'll do it; no, we won't. For instance, you might say, "Why don't we talk together about the possible places we might hold the winter sales conference. Then we'll each pick the three that sound best to us and see which sites get the most top choices."

The advantage of this method is that everyone's wishes

(or needs, or best answers) get clear recognition. The Staller is not put in the position of choosing from among them. The process itself has done that. In addition, the Staller can tell the loser (not you, of course), "Your idea came in second."

Link Your Plan to Values of Quality and Service.

Whenever possible, but only if it's true, point out why your preferred alternative has superior quality. Stallers are concerned about quality, and this alone may nudge them into a decision.

Similarly, try to link your solution to beneficial outcomes for staff, the family, your customers or clients, or the world in general. You are not likely to get as far by emphasizing the monetary savings your plan will yield, unless, of course, you also show how the money saved will be used to increase the quality of life or to help someone.

Stallers are easy to lie to—they want so much to believe in and trust people. I urge you not to take advantage of their gullibility, because if they ever learn the truth they're likely to feel seriously offended and can often be unforgiving.

Give Support After the Decision Is Made.

Just because you've wrung an "Oh, all right, go ahead" out of your Staller, don't relax immediately. The moment you leave the field, questions and doubts in your Staller's mind may arise. You may not have surfaced all of the barriers. You might have, unknowingly, pushed the Staller to give in momentarily, and he or she may take the answer back as soon as your immediate pressure has subsided.

For these reasons, it pays to plan some person-to-person follow-up contacts. Even if it's not your usual style, consider a phone call the next day. You might say, for example, "Just called to see if you had any second thoughts about meeting with the director about my raise." If doubts have been raised, move back to problem solving. If that appears unnecessary, end your conversation with, "Don, in my opinion, you've done the right thing." Don't leave out the "in my opinion," however. It's the agreement and support from another person that helps a Staller remain steadfast.

By making these follow-up contacts, you are giving

support and you provide a means for dispelling resistance or internal conflict that may have developed overnight.

If Possible, Keep Control.

If at all possible, keep the initiative for action in your own hands. In the best of all possible worlds, you would say, "Okay, this is my understanding of the situation—if I don't hear from you within ten days, we'll ship." Unfortunately, life doesn't often allow that luxury. Second best is to negotiate a time when a decision, or progress toward it, is to be expected. "Rita, is this all right with you? I'll drop by (or call you) next Thursday afternoon to see where things are. If everything has fallen into place, I'll pick up the order right then."

Stallers will put off until the last moment dealing directly with decision conflicts. If there is no "last possible moment," they'll procrastinate indefinitely. More importantly, if you have not negotiated a specific time for getting back into the picture, you will find yourself getting increasingly antsy. Staring at a telephone, waiting for it to ring, is not pleasant. Worse, two weeks later, when your tension has overwhelmed your fear of seeming overanxious or pushy, you will be at your least effective when you call. You also will probably communicate your tension to the Staller, which will bring out even more of that super-helpfulness that produced the indecisive behavior in the first place.

Watch for Staller Overloads.

Anyone can overload, then explode. When Stallers can't stand the pressure of internal conflict, they move to escape quickly from the situation. The angry, abrupt, and impulsive decisions that result can be hard to live with. I have a vivid memory of the explosion of a physician-administrator I'll call Dr. Tillson. He was known to his staff as a very aggressive and touchy man. "Don't cross him or disagree," I was told, "he just runs all over you." My own experience with him had been the opposite—he was kindly, country doctorish, very attentive. One day, however, I observed him under seige from two of his subordinates who were pressing him to resolve a conflict between them. At first, he patiently heard each side out, tried to get each to listen to the other, and suggested that neither party was entirely in the right. Suddenly, he became very red in the face, bounced out of his seat, and shouted, with obvious fury, "All right, you want me to decide, then I will. From now on the policy will be *no* leaves on Friday afternoon for ward chiefs. And that's it." To the best of my knowledge, he refused even to discuss this policy again, even though it created hardships for a number of the staff.

The lesson to be learned is this: Keep your eyes fixed on that Staller if attempts at persuasion are getting heavy. Look for these signs:

(1) a change in tone of voice or appearance that looks like it might mean annoyance, even outright anger.
(2) evidence of estrangement or withdrawal. Picking up a book, glancing through correspondence in the middle of a conversation, and falling asleep are blatant examples I have seen.

If you find yourself in the presence of an overloaded Staller, I suggest you do your best to get him or her completely out of the decision situation. Reach over, pick up your letter, application form, report, or whatever, and leave as gracefully as you can. You might say something like: "Mr. Christman, I really want to rethink the whole idea of my transferring to Miami. I'll get back to you in two days." Or "Mr. Smart, after listening to some of your questions, I'd like to do some more thinking about how we can make our services fit your needs. I'll call you in two weeks for another appointment." When you meet again with your Staller, you will be primed to work twice as hard at ferreting out the underlying issues.

If taking the pressure relief route seems too hasty, think about these consequences. First, when Stallers make impulsive decisions, they often refuse to reconsider them. Having once gotten off the horns of that dilemma, nothing will get them back on. Second, even if they seem to decide for you under pressure, their part in the implementation will be at arm's length and equivocal. You know what that can be like:

| YOUR BOSS: | "Mr. Harvey, my staff seems to think that it would be a good idea if we change the billing procedure." |
| HIS/HER BOSS: | "And what do you think?" |

YOUR BOSS: "Well, I, uh, guess that the old way
              always seemed to work. Of course, I'm
              all for improvements, but . . ."

COPING WITH STALLERS IN PRACTICE

I'd like to end this chapter with a note Janet sent me. It illustrates many of the steps I've been discussing. As you will see, she coped reasonably well with her stalling boss, and was quite tickled with herself for having done it.

When we had left them, Janet and Donna, her boss, were not speaking.

After three weeks of frustration, communication by note, and a real fear that I was going to lose a good job, I decided that I needed to do *something*. I stopped by at coffee break and asked Donna if she would have lunch with me. We went to a quiet little tea room where we'd be able to talk. After a bit, I said, "I don't know what's happened over the last few months, but something is wrong, and if I don't get some understanding of it, I don't think I'm going to make it. It would really help me now if you could tell me if there is something on your mind about my work." She didn't even pause in eating her soup as she said, "You've always been very responsible; you know how to work hard, and your ideas are tops."

When the situation has really gotten out of hand, it's wise to head for neutral ground.

Stallers usually listen well to openness in others.

Janet asks for help.

Donna has to work up to the bad news.

For some reason—probably a mixture of relief and not knowing what to say—I just nodded. Then, she started in again: "Well, Mr. Bennett (her boss) has asked some

Janet was lucky. If she had said, "Oh, I'm glad," Donna may have found it too painful to drop the bomb.

questions about the amounts of money that you've spent on some of your projects. It turns out that you've been spending more than anyone else in the unit." I managed to just sit and listen while my mind frantically moved to thoughts of where I could get another job. What I said was, "What do you suppose we ought to do?" And what do you know, she began to talk about some possible things. We decided that I would do a breakdown of where the money went on all my projects. That way I could point out something that I believed to be true (and it turned out that she believed it also, although she wasn't sure). I may *spend* more than other people, but my returns are greater as well. When the quarterly reports came in, I was right; Mr. Bennett was pleased, and I got a raise.

Mr. Bennett was probably rabid, but see how mildly it came out.

Problem-solving question and request for help rolled into one.

A lot of trouble would have been avoided if Donna had only asked. But that's what makes her a Difficult Person.

REVIEW OF COPING WITH STALLERS

—Make it easy for Stallers to tell you about conflicts or reservations that prevent the decision.
—Listen for indirect words, hesitations, and omissions that may provide clues to problem areas.
—When you have surfaced the issues, help Stallers solve their problems with the decision.
—At times the Staller's reservation will be about you. If so:
    acknowledge any past problem.
    state relevant data nondefensively.
    propose a plan.
    ask for help.
—If you are not part of the problem, concentrate on helping the Staller examine facts. Use the facts to place

alternative solutions in priority order. This makes it easier if the Staller has to turn someone else down.
—If real, emphasize the quality and service aspects of your proposal.
—Give support after the decision seems to have been made.
—If possible, keep the action steps in your hands.
—Watch for signs of abrupt anger or withdrawal from the conversation. If you see them, try to remove the Staller from the decision situation.

Chapter 9

TOWARD EFFECTIVE COPING: THE BASIC STEPS

Underlying the coping process are six fundamental steps that will help you cope successfully, no matter what type of Difficult Person you need to deal with. (1) Assess the situation. (2) Stop wishing the Difficult Person were different. (3) Get some distance between you and the difficult behavior. (4) Formulate a coping plan. (5) Implement your plan. (6) Monitor the effectiveness of your coping strategy, modifying it where appropriate. Let's look at each of these steps in turn.

ASSESS THE SITUATION

At work, as in the rest of life, we encounter many situations in which others seem to cause us difficulty. A co-worker turns grumpy and uncommunicative, the boss blows his stack over a minor mistake, subordinates may seem perpetually ready with new excuses about assignments still unfinished, and clients may act as if they know more about our business than we do. Which of these situations involve Difficult People? How do you recognize a Difficult Person when you see one?

The first preparatory step in the coping process is to

determine whether or not you are dealing with a Difficult Person or with a situation that is temporarily bringing out the worst in an ordinarily nondifficult person. A well-documented but often unrecognized human tendency is to become irritated over the foibles of others while excusing our own as "just being human." Whenever we run into a frustrating situation, or a "no" to an idea or wish, it is tempting enough to brand others as "difficult." But seeing Difficult People wherever you turn is likely to earn yourself the label you are placing on others—and it won't help you to cope with the situation.

Sometimes, deciding that you are in truth dealing with a Difficult Person is relatively simple. Your assistant who complains to you constantly about other staffers in a passive way will at once be recognized as a Complainer; the boss whose abrasive, hostile manner causes all of his or her subordinates to groan inwardly and turn grimly silent outwardly is a clear Sherman Tank. These are the individuals about whom office gossip revolves, individuals that most people agree are problem-causers.

Other troublesome encounters, however, are not so clear. When criticized by a boss for getting a report in late again, you may secretly feel that he or she has a right to feel angry. The steady customer who complains about the decline in service may have a legitimate beef. Or you may be confused about why your relationship with a neighbor began to deteriorate about six months ago. If coping is to be effective, we need some realistic measures by which to judge whether someone is truly a Difficult Person or a person caught up in an unfortunate but temporary situation.

In the Introduction, we said that the Difficult Person is one who acts chronically in a difficult manner. This is the litmus test of whether we are genuinely faced with a Difficult Person, whether we can look for a simpler solution to our poor relations, or whether we should take a closer look at the possibility that we are just seeking an easy excuse for our own problems. To make this test, use the answers to the following questions as guides:

(1) Has the person in question usually acted differently in three similar situations?
(2) Am I reacting out of proportion to what the situation warrants?

(3) Was there a particular incident that triggered the troublesome behavior?

(4) Will direct, open discussion relieve the situation?

If your answer to any one of these four questions is yes, chances are you are not primarily dealing with a Difficult Person, even if that person's behavior is now impossible. If your answers are all in the negative, then you probably are confronted with one. Let me elaborate and give some examples from my consulting experience of individuals who might have appeared on the surface to be Difficult People but who actually weren't.

Question 1: Has the Person in Question Usually Acted Differently in Three Similar Situations?

Carl was a first-line data processing supervisor who appeared to have all the earmarks of a Difficult Person. He was surly and unresponsive to an extreme. A few days before I was asked to try to help out, he had suddenly pushed his desk into a corner of the office and piled books so high on one side that it was almost impossible for anyone to see him. Others in the office were alarmed by his erratic behavior and feared what he would do next.

When I talked with other employees in the office, however, they all agreed that Carl used to act quite reasonably and had been a relatively easy person to get along with. Carl's bizarre behavior, it turned out, was the result of a chain of events which began with his rejection for promotion six months before. When he was passed over for promotion, Carl complained to his area's vice-president. The vice-president concluded that Carl had been unfairly treated, and he ordered the heads of his division to establish a training plan so that Carl would know what he had to do in order to move up in the ranks.

It was not surprising that among the division heads there was some resistance to implementing this plan. They were resentful of Carl for having gone over their heads to complain. And Carl, once his meeting with the vice-president became public knowledge, began to feel that others in the office were waiting for him to fail in order to justify their decision not to promote him. Anxious and angry over what seemed to him a cold and unsupportive atmosphere, Carl began to fall down on the job. He turned in his reports late, made silly mistakes, and reduced his contacts with others on the floor to the bare minimum. Moving his desk into the corner was merely the logical expression of his feelings of increasing isolation from and suspiciousness of others.

When this chain of events was untangled, Carl was able to vent his feelings to his own supervisor, who had been shunted to one side when the trouble with the brass had started. He was then transferred to a different division where his effectiveness on the job soon began to return to normal. Carl's problem behavior was primarily situational. Understanding the source of his upset and providing him with a fresh environment was enough to enable him to work effectively and smoothly with others. The clue that Carl wasn't really one of those Difficult People we have described, but rather one whose problems with others could be rather straightforwardly resolved, was that prior to the promotion dispute he had acted quite differently.

Question 2: Am I Reacting Out of Proportion to What the Situation Warrants?

The second question to ask yourself after a series of uncomfortable exchanges with another is whether or not, upon reflection, your own responses to the person seem excessive. If you find yourself reacting negatively to practically everything a particular individual does, it may be that you are responding to something quite specific about the individual, not a systematic pattern of difficult behavior. Consider the following example.

A regional administrator of a federal agency called on me to advise him on what should be done about his silent and unresponsive bureau chief. It had gotten to the point, the regional administrator told me, where everything his bureau chief did infuriated him. He would yell at and abrade his subordinate, but the bureau chief would just sit there and say nothing. Even over minor issues, the regional administrator would blow up at the man. Once, for instance, the bureau chief asked a simple procedural question, and the regional administrator immediately snarled, "Why don't you read what we send you; don't you ever pay attention to what's going on?"

I soon discovered, however, that there was a specific cause for the administrator's upset. He had recently sent the bureau chief instructions on how to handle an important policy meeting. The bureau chief proceeded to do just the opposite of what his boss had requested, and it wasn't long before the administrator heard about it. He stormed into the bureau chief's office and read him the riot act. The bureau chief just sat there in stony silence, then he got up and walked out of the room without saying a word.

As it turned out, and as the regional administrator himself was later to admit, the bureau chief had had very good reasons for altering his presentation at the conference. But because of his boss's approach, he never explained this to him, becoming increasingly unresponsive instead. The administrator, for his part, grew more and more furious because of his subordinate's lack of response. For the regional administrator, the clue that he might not be dealing with a Difficult Person should have been the degree to which he became upset with his bureau chief over subsequent, admittedly minor, matters.

Question 3: Was There a Particular Incident that Triggered the Troublesome Behavior?

The third question to ask yourself after a series of unpleasant incidents with an individual is whether or not there was a particular incident that triggered the difficult behavior. Frequently, posing this question becomes just another way of asking questions 1 and 2. In the above examples, Carl's lack of promotion was the trigger of his troublesome behavior, and the regional administrator's approach and the bureau chief's response to their meeting over the conduct of the policy conference was the spark of the bureau chief's subsequent behavior pattern. In these instances, and others like them, exposing and discussing openly the triggering incidents led to a reasonably productive resolution of the problem.

Question 4: Will Direct, Open Discussion Relieve the Situation?

After thinking through these assessment questions, you may suspect that you're faced with a relationship gone sour rather than with a Difficult Person. In that case, an attempt to untangle the problem through direct discussion with the other person is a useful next step. It, of course, may not alleviate the situation, but you will have satisfied yourself that, with awareness that you might be a part of the problem, you have done your best to work it through. These steps, modified to fit your own style and the circumstances, offer the best chance of success.

First, initiate a conversation, preferably by making an appointment to demonstrate your serious intent and lessen the chance of interruption. Open the conversation with a statement of your own sense that things have not been going well between you. Wait for a reaction. If none is forthcoming, try again with your best guess about an incident that may have opened the breech in your relationship.

In the case of that regional administrator and his bureau chief, it might sound like this: "Murry, I've been thinking about the way we've been getting on each other's nerves lately—did it start when I jumped on you about that policy meeting last January? Are there problems at home? What's happening?" Notice that your last question was open-ended. That will help you to deal with any uncertainty or reluctance in the other person using the steps described for Silent and Unresponsive People in Chapter 4.

If the response you get typifies any one of the Difficult People we've visited, and you can't shake him or her out of it by restating what you've just said, proceed with coping. If, however, he or she begins to open up to you, bringing up old slights, forgotten arguments, or neglected rewards, take pains to avoid explaining it all away. Do *not* give all of the reasons why you did those things that were seen as threatening or demeaning. You will be tempted to do just that, especially if you are of a matter-of-fact turn of mind. But nothing will kill your attempts at resolving the problem sooner than, "Oh, yes, well, you know that when you brought your promotion up at the annual performance review, we had a salary freeze and I couldn't bring it up later because . . ." Instead, as simply as you can, state what your intention was at that time and what it is now: "Well, I can see that what I did left you feeling that the extra work you did wasn't very important to me. That's certainly not what I wanted then, and it's not what I want now. What do we need to do to make sure that it doesn't happen again?" If it appears that what you've said hasn't registered, that is, it is followed by a restatement of those old grievances, try again. But, first, do as careful a job as you can of acknowledging both what's been said and the feelings behind it. Refer to the initial coping steps in Chapter 3 for suggestions on doing this effectively.

Once the conversation begins to turn toward preventing future accurrences, continue with it. Be ready, however, to acknowledge and then restate your own intentions if the conversation starts to slip.

STOP WISHING THEY WERE DIFFERENT

Perhaps the most valuable single step that anyone can take in preparation for coping with Difficult People is to *stop wishing they were different*. This is far easier said than done.

Think of someone standing over you, pounding the table, shouting and cursing at you. If you're like most people, you'll sit there muttering to yourself something like: "He shouldn't be that way!" or "Why is she acting that way? That's not the way *anyone* should be!" *Not* to feel abused, not to feel that the aggressor should be different, would seem almost out of the question. The problem is this. To the extent that you are sitting there trying to wish your tormenting frog into a prince (or princess) you will be that much *less* able to do just those things that might minimize that terrible behavior.

Blaming Isn't Changing.

In situations like the above, we blame something exclusively internal on the other person. We all tend to believe that others are basically like ourselves, that they have similar values, assumptions, and feelings. Consequently, when they do not act as we expect or would like, it is "logical" to assume that their unexpected and unwanted behavior must be due to hostile intentions, a faulty personality, or just plain personal "difficultness." As a result, we conclude that it is up to *them* to change.

Given this very human attribute, what else is there for us to do but plaintively wish that our Difficult Person were different and then feel frustrated when he or she doesn't change? The confounding fact is that Difficult

People at times behave rather well. This lends temporary credence to a belief that finally they've changed, only to have this credence undermined when the disliked behavior shows up again. Feeling virtuous and self-righteous for having "done all I can" is very understandable, but unfortunately it won't keep your interaction with that offensive person from falling into the same rut.

The source of the great strength with which this wish can take hold is that deeply buried sense of witching power that is left over from the childhood of each of us. The attempt is an exercise in futility that only sidetracks you from what you *can* do to alleviate the situation.

Giving Up the Magical Wish.

The second step toward successful coping, then, is to give up that magical wish. When you look closely, you are likely to be surprised at how much energy you had used in the wishing. Because it is such a valuable aid to coping, in the next few paragraphs I'll suggest some actions you can take to give up the wish that your own Difficult Person were different. Giving up the wish is a letting-go process. You will likely feel a sense of relief as you release this psychic wrestling hold that required great energy yet failed to make anything change.

To help yourself let go of that attempt at magical spell-casting, try to become aware of the strength of that fantasy-filled wish in your own life. It helps. You may feel it as a hope that "this time it will be different." Or it may turn up as that feeling of disappointment and dismay when Barbara, *again*, brings her order book in a day late. Well, why are you so surprised? Even more to the point, why did you tell your supervisor that you would have all the orders in on the same day you set for Barbara, when you knew she was always late?

What a bitter cycle: an unrealistic hope turns to resentment only to be followed by another unrealistic hope. To see yourself in that cycle playing a part that seems out of touch with the actuality of who Barbara is can help you to choose behaviors that will be more appropriate and more likely to gain for you a better, more productive relationship with her. It is with others as they are that you must learn to cope.

GET SOME DISTANCE BETWEEN YOU AND THE DIFFICULT BEHAVIOR

When confronted with Difficult People, we tend to become so wrapped up in the situation—wishing the individuals were different, feeling angry toward them, and upset at ourselves for being dragged into another unpleasant routine—that we're unable to think through more effective responses. Difficult People are difficult to us because they touch off a series of reactions in ourselves which always seem to become part of their game.

In order to be able to cope with Difficult People, to break the destructive patterns of behavior which you fall into with them, you must learn to gain some persepvice on their actions, even while they are talking to you. Only by seeing their patterns of behavior and understanding the source of those patterns will you be able to devise an effective strategy for coping with them.

Your goal is a detached and distanced view of that Difficult Person, while he or she is in the process of being difficult (even shortly thereafter may do). Here are some quotations from those who achieved this perspective with their own problem people: "I'm looking at her through the wrong end of a telescope; every detail clear, but very far away." "I can see him as if he were sitting in a cage with a label over him." "It's not just me he does this to—he's that way with everyone." "I suddenly saw that if I wait for her to stop complaining and start taking some action on her own, I'll wait forever."

To have a distanced perspective of someone does not mean being cold, unfeeling, or nonunderstanding. My own experience is that the opposite is often true, particularly with those I care about, or need, the most. A truism that usually holds here, too, is: the more you can see others as truly separate from yourself, the more you are able to see them as they are.

Labeling Can Help.

Most people feel an inner resistance to the idea of categorizing people, putting them in boxes labeled "Difficult People," "Indecisive," "Complainer," or whatever. Human beings are immensely complex and adaptable, and no one can be completely reduced to any category. But that doesn't mean that there aren't some very practical reasons for categorizing people. One of these is that labeling people often helps you feel "distanced" from them, especially if they're people with whom you're very involved.

It allows you to see their behavior as happening outside of yourself and your personal responses. That is, it often enables you to see that the Hostile-Aggressive person or the Complainer isn't being hostile or complaining just with you, but that he or she does this to everyone in similar situations. Identifying the kind of Difficult Person you've encountered can in itself help you to take the disturbing behavior less personally. You become less paralyzed wondering what *you* did to bring it on and become more ready for an active, more effective response.

Another practical reason for categorizing people is that by doing so you may gain an insight into their behavior. Regardless of any other attributes they may have, Indecisives have learned to act the way they do because it gets them through, or out of, some kinds of situations. Thus, just recognizing that they are habitually indecisive tells you something about them.

I'm suggesting, then, that while you are doing your business with people who are driving you up a tree, you actively try to think about them in some category of "Difficult Person." It is important, however, that you see the labels and the behavior patterns they describe as *prototypes* rather than *stereotypes*. Using "Complainer" as a stereotype label would imply that all Complainers are alike, a statement far from the truth. What we mean by that label is rather that all Complainers show certain behaviors in common, but in most other ways they are quite different.

Looking at people as if they were specimens does, I think, cut down on spontaneity. Done to extreme, as a means of avoiding intimacy, for example, it is as harmful as being submerged in a relationship. This book is about coping, however, not being spontaneous; for coping a degree of "outside" perspective does seem to help. The purpose of this attempt to gain distance is not to write off your own responsibility for any situation but to free yourself for a more productive and, in the long run, more caring response.

Understanding Can Help.

For achieving a broader perspective on a Difficult Person, it does seem to help to *believe* that you understand what it's like to be one. When you can make some sense out of behavior that has previously seemed nonsensical, you feel less confused and helpless—more able to cope.

The kind of understanding that I am suggesting here is "understanding from the inside," to use psychologist George Kelly's term. Think of that someone who has continued to do those frustrating and awful things in the face of negative reactions, hints, resignations, and even open warfare. The task is to imagine how life looks to that person, and to relate that perspective to comparable experiences of your own life.

Gaining and maintaining this kind of understanding is devilishly hard. Can we ever fully succeed with any other person? I doubt it. But even a snatch of such understanding can provide the necessary vantage point that will release you from those patterns of interaction that bring out the worst in everyone.

FORMULATE A PLAN FOR INTERRUPTING THE INTERACTION

Once you have managed to gain some distance and some understanding of the Difficult Person's behavior, it is time to devise a strategy for coping more effectively with it. The basic tenet that underlies successful coping is a simple but often overlooked fact: the behavior of human beings is highly interactional. Because this fact is often forgotten, most of us are cut off from a source of leverage in our relationships with Difficult People that is there for the using. To see how and why this leverage works, consider the following two possible scenarios that might unfold when I get up to give a talk before a group.

Two Cycles of Behavior.

Suppose, in the first instance, that I am addressing a group of supervisors who, unknown to me, have been ordered by their superior to drop everything and come hear me speak. They're resentful of having to take time out from other chores to listen to me, and, under the circumstances, they're not initially interested in my topic.

After I've been talking only a few minutes, I begin to notice that some of the supervisors are nodding off while others are squirming in their chairs or staring out the window. They may be inwardly fuming at what an S.O.B. their boss is for making them come to this meeting and wondering how they'll still be able to make tomorrow's production deadline, but I don't know that. What I notice is widespread boredom and disinterest, which I interpret as solely a response to my speech, and as a consequence begin to feel defensive and self-conscious about my presentation. My voice tightens up, I start stumbling over words, and my delivery begins to sound more tentative. The supervisors notice this change in my presentation. Most become even more irritated with me, now having even more evidence that their resentment at having been forced to attend was well founded. A few, perhaps, may start to feel sorry for me and ask forced questions in an effort to prop me up. But both the visible irritation of the majority and the over-solicitousness of the minority make me feel even more self-conscious. Chances now are great that both I and my presentation will provoke even more irritation and boredom among my audience. Increasingly more tense and disconcerted, I expend more and more energy trying to gain my audience's approval, less and less on the substance of my speech. Thus, I progress to the lowest level of my competency. Later on, perhaps, while trying to understand this disaster I will salve my feelings with the thought that I was faced with an unruly, unappreciative, and completely difficult group.

The above scenario is an example of what I call a *negative interaction cycle*. An initial negative encounter between myself and the audience spiralled into increasingly negative and unproductive interactions between us. Without doubt, the particular ways in which I responded to the seat squirming and evidence of disinterest was determined by who I am—my personality and my repertoire of learned responses—but it was something in the specific character of that situation that elicited that set of increasingly incompetent responses (tightening up, etc.) from me.

Now let's look at a contrasting scenario, one that involves a *positive interaction cycle*. Suppose that a few minutes into my talk one of the supervisors remarks that he doesn't know about the others, but as far as he is concerned, what I am saying makes a lot of sense to him and he's eager to hear more. My initial feelings of discomfort begin to diminish, I start to relax, my voice becomes lively, and my tone sounds more self-confident. Others in the group begin to worry less about their deadlines as they pay more attention, perhaps become intrigued by what I am saying, and I, noticing this, begin to feel more relaxed. I am now able to devote full attention to presenting the substance of my talk in an effective manner.

In this instance, the interaction between myself and my audience cycled in a positive direction. Once again, I responded to the audience in the way that I did because I have my particular personality, developed through my own unique past experiences. This time, however, because of an affirming note early in the speech, the outcome was quite different. The cast of characters in these two scenarios is the same. What makes the difference is the quality of the interaction.

Let me put what I've been saying a little more abstractly. The way people behave is not due solely to an early learned set of personality traits, although personality traits certainly have much to do with anyone's behavior. Nor is behavior purely a response to the particular situations in which people find themselves, although it is certainly true that any person will respond differently in different circumstances. There is always a relationship between an individual's personality and the specific situation the person is in, as that person sees it.

Here's the way it works. Personality is simply the repertoire of strategies and tactics for dealing with life that an individual has learned to prefer. Any specific situation at times pulls out and at times inhibits certain of the strategies in that person's armentarium. When my audience acted bored and disinterested, it pushed a "respond" button in me. The question is why did I tighten up, blame myself, but pretend outwardly that nothing was happening, rather than remain calm, suspect that the members of the audience had other things on their minds, and inquire matter-of-factly, or with humor, what the difficulty was. My ability to consistently do the latter increased markedly when I was helped to see that, early on, I had learned to blame myself when others became irritated with me, had developed a very strong need for group approval, and, even worse, had learned that it was improper to comment on what others seemed to think of me. These insights, however, came later. I would not have survived my earlier years on the "seminar circuit" if I had not frequently encountered the second scenario when, certain of at least one member's approval, more positive and productive responses were elicited from me.

What makes a Difficult Person different from the rest of us is that he or she is more likely to respond in ways that manage to get the worst out of everyone. We can all be negative and unproductive in various situations, but defensive, unproductive behavior in the Difficult Person is more frequent, more easily elicited, and at a lower threshold than for the rest of us. What makes it possible to cope with Difficult People at all is that, like everyone else, they have positive responses in their repertoire. If you can learn to avoid doing and saying those things that elicit the negative behavior from a Difficult Person and structure the interaction so as to encourage his or her positive, more productive responses, then you will be coping more successfully with that individual.

The Leverage Is in the Interaction.

The primary leverage you have for coping with the difficult behavior of other people is your ability to change the nature of the interaction you are both caught in. You can do this by changing your own piece of it, your own behavior. To do this properly, as we discussed earlier in the chapter, you must mentally step outside the interaction long enough to see that your own behavior was elicited from you by what the other person has done, or at least by what you thought he or she had done.

You are free to change your part in the interaction precisely because you no longer wait for those difficult others to do the remedying. Let me take as an example those wonderfully nice people we met in Chapter 5 who promise you anything but don't deliver. Don't you have a right to expect that those people will be honest with you, that they will say, "I cannot have that report in by Thursday, other things have priority," rather than, "Sure, Thursday will be fine"? Of course you do. Everyone has a right to expect that the people they associate with will be candid. The problem is that those overagreeable people just *can't* be blunt, unless you give them a lot of help. You could emphatically insist on your right to get honest answers, driving those poor overagreeable persons into a panic. Or you can choose to do the work of changing the situation yourself so as to make it easier for the truth to emerge.

IMPLEMENT YOUR STRATEGY

Once you have determined an appropriate plan of attack, the obvious next step toward successful coping is to implement it. Here are some general guidelines on timing and preparation.

Timing.

You should choose the moment to implement your strategy with some discretion. There are two main criteria of proper timing. First, you should select a period when the Difficult Person is not overburdened with other problems. For example, if the individual has just been given a huge assignment or just had a run-in with the boss or just separated from his or her mate, it is best to delay putting your plan into effect. When people are under a lot of stress, they tend to be less resilient in their responses to new developments, and will be less likely to react to your confrontation in a fruitful manner. By disrupting their established patterns of behavior when they are under great stress, you also risk their taking their frustrations over that recent separation or fight with the boss out on you.

The second criterion of appropriate timing is whether or not you have the time yourself, and the energy, to carry through with your coping plan. You don't want to confront the Difficult Person once and then seem to fall back because you no longer are able to devote the necessary effort to the interaction between you. Successful coping depends on your ability to pay careful and systematic attention to what happens between you and the Difficult Person. Your attempts to interrupt the interaction between the two of you may not work on the first or second or even third try. A Difficult Person's patterns of habitual response tend to be deeply ingrained, and it may take them awhile to react to your new behavior and develop a new way of responding to it.

Preparation.

While my experience has been that the coping methods explained in this book usually work even if they are not carried out with great skill, if you can, it will pay to practice your strategy before actually confronting that Difficult Person. This is especially true with Sherman Tanks, Snipers, and Bulldozers. Practicing what you intend to say in front of a mirror is an effective form of preparation. Be sure to say the words aloud. Perhaps an even better method is to corral a friend or your spouse to go through a dry run with you, playing the role of the Difficult Person. Ready yourself for an abrasive encounter by imagining that Difficult Person standing in front of you shouting or swearing. Then say the coping words as well as you can. Try to visualize the encounter developing just as you hope it will. If your image of a successful interchange falters, start over.

MONITOR THE PROGRESS OF YOUR COPING AND MODIFY WHEN APPROPRIATE

Once you have begun implementing your coping plan, it is important to monitor its effects carefully and modify it if necessary. You may discover, for instance, that your approach has little or no influence because you have misinterpreted the kind of Difficult Person you are confronted with. You may have mistaken, for example, Super-Agreeable behavior for Indecisive. In such a case, there's nothing for it but to heave a sigh and devise a new strategy.

It's also possible that no matter what you do, your attempts at coping will fail to produce many productive results. This may happen because the threshold at which the difficult behavior is triggered is so low that you would have to become a slave to the moods and idiosyncracies of the Difficult Person in order to avoid triggering that defensive behavior. It also may happen because the person is so engrossed in his or her own inner life that what you do in the present has little effect on his or her behavior. For instance, they may explode because of some thought of their own which is unrelated to anything you have said or done. In such circumstances, further attempts to cope would appear clearly counterproductive. When should you abandon coping attempts, and what should you do then?

When to Abandon the Coping Effort.

My advice is first to try to cope with the Difficult Person using the methods proposed in the previous chapters, and any others you can invent. Expect to have to persist, plan, and become as skillful as you can, because you are the one supplying the energy and motivation. But if your attempts at coping don't work, literally get as much distance from the Difficult Person as you can. Don't wait two years to ask for a transfer away from that difficult boss, try to arrange it before the interaction has taken too great a toll on both of you. You may both benefit from the change.

The best kind of distance to get from that troublesome other is the easiest and least costly kind. Here are some examples.

Physical Distance. Walk away, leaving the scene of action; get yourself transferred to another office; obtain a divider for the office so that at least you don't have to look at the person (and he or she won't have to look at you).

Organizational Distance. Move the Difficult Person to a staff position, with no authority over others; transfer yourself into another unit; ask for a different committee assignment.

When considering whether or not to abandon your coping attempts, it is important to remain flexible and not let your pride determine your decision. Acknowledging that your efforts at coping have failed can be a source of wounded pride. You may be tempted to try again, and again, because you can't bear the thought of not being successful at everything you try or because it has become a point of pride for you not to back down from, for instance, a Hostile-Aggressive type. But consider whether, like Dean Edwards in the example below, the benefit of saving that modicum of pride is worth the torment of having to remain in the vicinity of an impossible person.

Dean Edwards was a young, very able project chief in a large organization. Anathema to him was Lee Jackson, the organization's administrative chief, who habitually ignored him in meetings, "overlooked" decisions made by the head of the organization that were favorable to Dean's project, "ordered" Dean's boss to keep Dean away from him, and publicly questioned the value of Dean's project in a sarcastic manner.

After a year and a half of acute distress, Dean, with his boss's approval, designated one of his staff, an older man, as "Project Administrative Officer" and assigned all contact with Lee to this person. During the following two years the project was able to get its most needed administrative support. Dean recognized that he had, in a sense, given in to Lee at some cost to both his ego and his "strong man" image. However, his freedom from debilitating attacks of tension seemed clearly to outweigh those costs.

Remember, *no one* is under a moral obligation to remain in the vicinity of, to keep working with, or even to keep living with, another person whose behavior is demoralizing, severely upsetting, or stress-producing. I emphasize this point because I keep finding people for whom it is not obvious at all. They confuse a practical question of costs and benefits with a moral imperative.

Without doubt, getting yourself, or that Difficult Person, out of the situation *may* be too costly in terms of unmet needs, thwarted ambitions, or pain to those you care about. You may like your job and have few alternatives anyway; you may need to get along with that boss or that manager in order to move into a better position in the company; you may feel a sense of responsibility for your patients even though you can't stand the director of the clinic. The fact that many times we are, to one degree or another, forced to come to terms with Difficult People is what makes learning how to cope with them useful and necessary.

Chapter 10

THINKING STYLES: AN ADDED DIMENSION IN COPING WITH OTHERS

In the preceding chapters I have presented seven of the most difficult patterns of behavior and how to cope with them. There are, of course, many variations within categories—all Complainers, Baloons, and Stallers are not the same, for example—and there are many variations in what each of us brings to those encounters with difficult others.

Take Sherman Tanks, for instance. Some are quite aware of the havoc they create, others are not. Some seem like impersonal juggernauts, others have a "mean" quality to them. Some will use physical force, others not. To fully understand these differences we would need a detailed and multidimensional map of how and when each of these people developed his or her set of strategies and thinking patterns. To understand the idiosyncracies of each of our own approaches to Difficult People and what exact strategy would work best, we would need equally detailed maps. The purpose of this chapter is to provide the ingredients for just that kind of mapping.

Anyone's behavior is so broadly based and so deep that no single explanatory scheme now available can make usable sense of it all. However, by building on the work of others, Allen Harrison and I, with the help of our associates, have developed a framework which, while it doesn't pretend to explain everything, still can add some useful depth to coping with others. (Those of you who wish to learn more about thinking styles will find some suggested readings listed in the Reference section at the end of the book.) This framework is based on two assumptions. The first assumption is that there *is* a profound connection between the way a person has learned to think about the world and the way that person behaves. The second assumption is that there are a limited number of ways of thinking about things. Both of these assumptions have empirical, experimental and common-sense evidence to support them. *Thinking Styles* is the term we have come to use to refer to the particular ways of gathering data and making decisions that we have identified. The uniqueness in each of us lies in the way we combine these thinking styles to think about whatever it is that we think about.

Learning your own and others' characteristic styles of thinking can enrich and refine your understanding of the difficult behavior of others and point up the best way to cope with disruptive interactions that may arise. Specifically, understanding your thinking style and that of the Difficult Person you are confronted with can help you cope in these specific ways:

(1) Knowing more about yourself will help you to adapt the methods described in the foregoing chapters to your own ways of thinking and acting.
(2) This framework for understanding others can help you develop your own coping approach to people who are difficult but who don't seem to fit any of the categories covered in chapters 2 through 8.
(3) Thinking styles of those who ordinarily aren't difficult can clash. It helps to be alerted to the explosive mixtures that occur when certain types of people get together. If you're aware of potential problems you can head them off, minimize their effects, or at least get ready to duck.

THINKING SITUATIONALLY

To understand the concept of thinking styles, consider two people, Sally and Milt, each faced with the task of finding a job.

Sally starts her quest by doing a careful analysis of her financial and occupational needs. She obtains a list of potential employers in the area and surveys her own wants and abilities. She next develops a systematic plan for discovering all the suitable positions that may be available, and methodically executes her strategy. Sally then waits patiently until all the replies are in before following up on those that best meet her criteria.

Milt, on the other hand, begins to look for work by energetically calling his friends and acquaintances, asking if they know of possible openings. He peruses the newspaper want-ads and looks to see which civil service exams might be open. Milt responds at once, and competently, to whatever opportunities pop up. As soon as he finds a prospective employer who appreciates his drive and energy, and perhaps offers a chance for rapid advancement, he takes the job. Never mind that another, better possibility *might* turn up.

To get what they wanted Sally and Milt thought differently about the same task. They looked for different kinds of information, weighed it differently, and came up with different conclusions. And so do we all. Although we have all learned many ways to use information and draw conclusions from it, most of us, like Sally and Milt, have preferences for one or two styles of thinking. These thinking styles largely determine the kinds of questions we ask, what we do with the answers, how we go about making decisions—indeed, much of our outlook on life.

What style of thinking is best? There's no simple answer to this question. Any thinking style is a strength or a liability depending upon where it's used and how much it's used. For example, Sally's orderly and methodical way of thinking was an undoubted strength. Milt could have used some, certainly. But Sally spent so much time developing more and more detailed plans that she missed out on some great opportunities, not to mention the fact that she bored her friends to tears.

But when the situation calls for moving fast, grabbing your hat and being the first in line, Milt's rapid response to the news of the moment is clearly a strength. His problem is that he doesn't stop for a bit of orderly, logical analysis at the right moment. That's why Milt's friends shake their heads and sigh once again over the way he wastes his talents on jobs he rushes into that later turn out to be unsuited to his talents or temperament.

Different situations call for different ways of thinking and acting. Be tough, accurate, and fact-conscious when needed; be loose, speculative, or tender at other times. This truth has been pointed out for millennia. But being situationally responsive is not often associated with the condition of being human (at least in Western society). We ought to learn how to be highly adaptive to changing circumstances, but most of us haven't.

The unfortunate reality is that most of us (about 85 percent, according to our data) tend to use the same

approaches over and over again, regardless of the requirements of the situation. And why not? We've learned to
think the way we do because in some way it has worked
for us, with the kind of rapid, intermittent rewarding as
children that drives any kind of learning deep into our
core. What, then, could be more natural than our responding to demanding situations by taking the same tack
we know has worked in the past?

When our cerebral winds fit the situation, the benefits
can be great; the costs arise when the situation changes
and we can't. As you will see in the thumbnail descriptions that follow, the liabilities that accrue to any thinking
style are often nothing more than too much of a good
thing, applied without regard to the situation. For example, those creative people who have a feel for the
complexity of real-life situations, who can see truth in
all sides of a problem, are gems. But when they sidle
around, arguing each side of an issue, never coming to a
conclusion, a potential value rapidly becomes an actual
headache.

FIVE STYLES OF THINKING

Harrison and I have found it useful to distinguish five
main styles of thinking: Synthesist, Idealist, Pragmatist,
Analyst, and Realist. These names and the style descriptions to follow were developed for use in conjunction with
a questionnaire called the "Inquiry Mode Questionnaire:
Preferences in Ways of Asking Questions and Making
Decisions" (I₀Q for short).* We developed and tested
this instrument to measure actual differences in thinking
and conceptual strategies demonstrated by others and, in
part, to understand how individually competent people
could make very poor decisions. We have found it of
extraordinary use in assisting both individuals and work
groups in improving their effectiveness in making decisions.

The brief descriptions that follow will ask you to look
at "Synthesists," "Realists," and so forth. Keep in mind
that there is no such animal. The Label always means

* Further information on the use of this test can be obtained
from Bramson, Parlette, Harrison and Associates, 2140 Shattuck
Avenue, Suite 1210, Berkeley, CA 94704.

"to the extent that a person has learned to use and prefer the Synthesist approach to thinking." In fact, not one of us is all "Idealist" or all "Realist" or all anything. We have all learned to use all five of these approaches. For this reason, we all, at least to some extent, have the capacity to behave situationally. One situation might pull out of you, to the extent that you have learned it, a Synthesist approach, while another will elicit more of whatever Analyst thinking strategies you have learned. Later on we'll touch on compatibilities between persons. For now, try to visualize the essence of each thinking orientation.

The Synthesist.

The Synthesist orientation is based on a world view that there is no such thing as basic agreement among people about facts. What is important are the inferences that people make from the data they get, and the way those people feel about them. The "pure" Synthesist—if one existed—would believe that for two people to agree about any subject, they must first track the subject down to some basic value they both acknowledge to be the "essence" (a favorite Synthesist word) of the issue. Obviously, this can be a time-consuming process, which will bore non-Synthesists to distraction. Synthesists, then, are by nature debaters. They argue excessively. Not so much to win, but for the simple "fun" of arguing. They therefore can be maddening to people who would rather be straightforward. Synthesists tend to be challenging people, curious, restless, and creative. They are motivated to understand, but not necessarily control, the world and are much concerned that others see them as competent and worthy of admiration. They can be negative and disruptive, argumentative and rambling as they try to integrate different perspectives. A company president, for instance, had a habit of putting two or three staff members to work on the same research project—without telling any of them that others were looking into the same thing. When the staff reported in, of course, they were often flying very different kites. Each staff member had looked at different data and had made different recommendations based on differing assumptions. Once the truth was out, the president was accused of "duplicating

work" and of "encouraging conflict." Of course, both
accusations are valid, especially the latter. Harder to see,
but equally true, the president made creative use of the
conflict. The solutions that he finally chose were an
integration of the differing reports.

The Idealist.

Unlike Synthesists, Idealists believe that people can
agree about anything if their differing views can be brought
together under the umbrella of a common goal or a
mutual ideal. Idealists often talk about goals and higher
values. They are open to many alternatives or suggestions
for action, and they are receptive to many differing views.
What they strive for is an agreement that will suit everyone. Idealists' occasional inflexibility arises from an insistence that the agreement for a plan of action, whatever
it is, must have high standards. Of course, those standards
are ones that match the personal values of the Idealist.
Idealists tend to expect much of themselves and of others.
At the same time, their deeply felt needs to be helpful
to others, to be appreciated, and to be found worthy of
trust make Idealists frequently very supportive and helpful to others. They can be so helpful, in fact, that occasionally they're just plain meddlesome.

Nurses, as one might expect, tend to have strong
Idealist orientations, as do teachers, social workers, and
others in the helping professions. Dora, the head of nursing in a large hospital in a Rocky Mountain state, is an
example. When the need for a budget cut came along
and she was asked not to fill eight existing vacancies, her
response was, "But what will happen to patient care?"
Dora couldn't accept the idea that a hospital might have
immediate financial needs that could outweigh her goals
for patient care. She accused the budget officer (an
Analyst) of being unfeeling and hard-hearted, interested
only in cutting costs. She delayed acting on requests that
she make the present staff work more efficiently and
revise procedures or tighten schedules. Dora was simply
displaying the characteristics of an Idealist under stress.
At the end of one meeting, as she walked down the hall
grumbling righteously, others on the staff were heard accusing her of being a "crusader," just as a high Idealist
ought to expect now and then.

The Pragmatist.

The main concern of Pragmatists is getting on with the job. They want to feel active and busy. Not necessarily with an eye toward long-lasting or ideal results, but to make do with what is available. Sometimes, simply, to get from here to there. Pragmatists' basic world view is that projects happen incrementally, in a piecemeal fashion. As planners they tend to advocate a contingency view, the basic element of which is "It all depends." Pragmatists are impatient with complex analyses and theorizing over the relationship of today's activities to distant goals. What can be done *right now* is all that one can be sure about. The Pragmatist "knows" that is the way the world works.

In day-to-day situations, Pragmatists are likely to be good at knowing what people will "buy." They can afford to approach problems in innovative or compromising ways because they have no vested interests in particular theories or methods. They provide optimism and enthusiasm that motivates people to move ahead even when the task seems mountainous. Because they don't need to take on the whole world at once, Pragmatists often have a high tolerance for ambiguity. They need less structure and predictability than the rest of us.

Tillie was a case in point. She found herself, one spring day, with a suddenly ill husband, a demanding job, and four children of assorted ages. While others close to her were overwhelmed by just the thought of the demands on her, Tillie remained calm and took each task as it came. She didn't work out complex plans for caring for the children, as her mother urged, in case John was going to be down for a long time. She dealt with each day and week one at a time and stayed afloat until her husband recovered enough to help out.

The Analyst.

To their critics, Analysts are stubborn, dogmatic, narrow-minded, compulsive, and detail-oriented (recall the hospital budget officer who drew Dora's righteous wrath). Analysts are often characterized by other, more freewheeling types as "straight-line thinkers." Once their thought processes have started on a line of thinking it is hard for them to deviate, even in the fact of contrary evidence. It is precisely this quality which is the Analyst's great strength and glaring weakness.

The Analyst's world view rests on an assumption that the world is basically orderly, logical, and rational. If it isn't, it should be, and Analysts will do their best to make it so. Within this world they have a need to feel competent and self-sustaining. Analysts believe "So long as we proceed carefully and methodically, things will work out." They are interested, above all else, in finding the correct method for getting something done. Analysts are apt to look for (or already "know") the "one best way" to solve a problem.

Given their analytical, logical approach, Analysts are likely to have a mathematical bent. Sometimes they carry too far their belief that most problems can be calculated or "figured out" through logical deduction. They look so hard for logical solutions that they have a hard time, sometimes, acknowledging anything that seems to them illogical—other people, for instance. Synthesists with their "far-out" suggestions and Idealists with their seeming over-concern for how people feel are especially incomprehensible.

Analysts can be very frustrating to Pragmatists when they insist on the "best" method in situations where a wide variety of alternative methods might do, some of which are more palatable to staff, clients, or customers than the "most efficient" one. Sally's job-hunting procedure, with which we opened this chapter, demonstrates the best and worst of the Analyst orientation.

The Realist.

What underlies Realists' orientation is an empirical world view. By that, I mean that to Realists, whatever can be seen, felt, heard, smelled, and experienced is vividly real. Anything else is somewhat fanciful, theoretical, and not very compelling. Realists assume that the world is as they sense it, the facts are there for everyone to see, and any two *intelligent* people can't help but agree on these facts. In that respect, the Realists are quite the opposite of Synthesists. They are bothered by compromise, synthesis, analysis, and idealism. They want to achieve concrete results: nothing else can influence the course of that "real world."

Because they are often forceful, hard-driving people, Realists tend to be impatient with high Analysts. When one succeeds the other in a position of authority, the results can be quite devastating. In one research firm, for example, the former president, who had been there for many years, had accustomed his staff to careful, detailed analytical work. He had expected reports to be thoroughly documented, carefully organized, and backed up with a great deal of detailed planning and statistics. The staff had become used to the Analyst approach.

When Mark took over, he took one look at the first reports on his desk, and threw up his hands. "Look," he said to his senior staff, "when you give me a report, I want one page that tells me what's to be done, when, with what results, and how much it will cost. You're the experts. I expect you to take care of detail. And another thing, when I give you an assignment I don't want to wait forever for an answer. I want time deadlines cut in half for projects, more production, and not one iota more analysis than is actually needed." It took a year of constant conversation for the company to adjust to Mark. For him it was a period of mounting frustration and impatience, as his staff grumbled underground about his impulsiveness and his need to "control." Two senior staff members were abruptly fired during the second month; however, the company eventually made the transition and went into a period of rapid and profitable growth.

Coping with Less Common Types of Difficult Behavior.

With the I.Q framework, you now have a system for understanding difficult behavior patterns that were not covered in chapters 2 through 8. Here, for example, is Indecisive A, a difficult person we have not yet met. The A stands for Analyst, of course. Perhaps not as frustrating as the big guns we visited in chapters 2 through 8, but a considerable nuisance for all that.

Indecisive A's differ considerably from their Staller counterparts described in Chapter 8. The problem behavior of Indecisive A is almost always focused on a piece of paper—a letter, a memo, or a short report you have brought in, knowing that it only needs a quick review and a pro forma approval. Not a big deal. No policy issues involved. Back you come the next day, but it isn't ready.

"That's funny," you say to yourself, "there weren't any problems; what's the delay?" Days, even weeks go by. Still no response. Nothing but bewilderment and frustration on your part.

What happened? Why, you've given that memo to a person with a predominantly Analyst thinking style. To one with that careful mind, any assignment, no matter how small, requires a systematic, even cautious analysis and review. Prior memos have to be read, books skimmed, standard operating procedures need to be consulted. Needless to say, this takes time, which the busy Analyst has little of. So, where does your memo go? Right! Into the pending basket it drops, where it "pends" until time is available (hah)!

To cope with those whose thinking styles pose problems for you, use a strategy analogous to those presented throughout this book: Flow with the same strengths that cause the trouble in order to minimize it. Here's how this would work with Indecisive A's. The same qualities that make Indecisive A's occasionally overanalytical also make them very responsive to any "structuring" you can apply to the situation, especially the establishment of a time framework. Thus, when you come flying in with your memo, take a minute to say, "I'll need to get that to the accounting office to meet their Thursday deadline." You might also set or ask for a specific time for a "rapid" review. Saying, "I'll be in Monday at 2:00 to see if there are any questions to be resolved," provides a time frame within which A's can be as analytical as they need to be.

When faced with an Analyst, nothing will keep your memo or letter in that pending basket longer than a calculation error or a loose and sloppy format. While Realists will overlook a careless error or a typo, correcting it themselves (with very black ink, naturally), A's become doubtful of the whole project. This, in turn, decreases the likelihood that you will be asked to do the reworking, since your carelessness has already been established. Your report will have to be sent for additional review to a third party that the A trusts.

An easy, but often erroneous assumption, given the sometimes gruff, noneffusive manner of some Analysts (those with low preference for Idealist or Pragmatist thinking styles, of course), is that delay in approval means a pocket veto. Certainly, that can and does happen. But at least as often, the delay is a concomitant of the A's need for thorough investigation. The danger of assuming that delay means denial is that you may start pushing, or worse, become emotional. Nothing will be more likely to evoke genuine resistance in your Indecisive A (remember the handy make-a-Negativist-kit described in Chapter 6). Once again, a planned time for a review can help keep you in the action rather than on the outside waiting and fuming.

ACKNOWLEDGING YOUR OWN THINKING STYLES

This is not a self-development book. Even so, let me suggest that acknowledging your own predominant styles, with their strengths and liabilities, helps in a number of ways. For instance, predominantly Realists, aggressive themselves, have the easiest time learning to stand up to Sherman Tanks; Idealists, who become immobilized or enraged by the sheer impropriety of Sherman Tanking, have the toughest. It helps to know in advance where you're going to find the going most difficult. This way, you don't feel so overwhelmed and defeated when it turns out to be such hard work.

Here are some other combinations that may give you trouble, depending on your own predominant mode of thought.

—Analysts and Realists get *impatient* with Complainers who seem so passive.
—Idealists are offended by Super-Agreeables, who seem more superficial than they really are.
—Realists (recall Janet in Chapter 8) want to shake, run over, and go around Indecisives.
—Analysts make Stallers even more of a problem by piling data on them, instead of helping them to open up with underlying issues.
—Pragmatists try to "live with" Sherman Tanks and Snipers and consequently frequently get eaten for breakfast.

Discovering Your Preferred Styles.

How do you discover your own customary approach to problems? Psychological movies to the contrary, there is substantial evidence that the best way to find out about people is to ask them about themselves. Measurement tools such as our I.Q Questionnaire merely provide some structured help to focus your attention on aspects of yourself that you're usually not aware of.

You can get a reasonable approximation by doing the following:

(1) Take a blank piece of paper and write the names of the five styles across the top.

(2) Reread the sections of the book that describe the five thinking styles.

(3) As you read each section write a number from 1 to 5 to rank each style of thinking—which style is most characteristic of your thinking, which is least characteristic, and the degrees in between. Use 5 for most characteristic and 1 for least characteristic.

(4) As you proceed through each section, change the number you have already assigned if it seems appropriate. You may have ranked Idealist as 5, for instance, but as you reread the Analyst section, you realize that this is a little more accurate description of you. Simply change the Idealist 5 to a 4 and assign 5 to Analyst.

When you're through, your paper may look like this:

Synthesist	Idealist	Pragmatist	Analyst	Realist
2	4	3	5	1

This would mean that, at least as far as you can tell, you are most likely to use the Analyst and Idealist strategies in dealing with life's problems. You are least likely to approach problems from the perspective of a Synthesist or Realist. The Pragmatist style is reasonably available to you. It will tend to keep you in touch with the everyday needs of yourself and others.

Adapt the Methods to Your Own Style.

There are ways and ways of doing anything. In describing the coping methods in the preceding chapters I've tried to get down the essence of each method. For best results, you should adapt them to fit with your own preferred styles of thinking. Here are some examples:

(1) You have predominantly an Idealist or Pragmatist

orientation and you recognize that standing up to a Sherman Tank, face-to-face, is just not your cup of tea. A workable adaptation of the standing-up-to approach, but not provoking or fighting, is to correspond by mail. You might write this note, for instance: "Peter, I didn't say anything at the meeting this noon, but I have to tell you that twice when I was about to make a point, you seemed to cut me off. My belief right now is that we did not fully explore the topic, can we schedule another meeting?"

While a written message doesn't have the immediacy of an on-the-spot response, it does have its own advantage: you have time to get your nerve up *and* you can choose your words carefully.

(2) You have a high preference for the Synthesist and/or Realist orientations. Your boss is a Bulldozer. Even thinking about doing your homework carefully and having the patience to move slowly makes your neck muscles spasm. The adaptation for you to consider is teaming up with others. First, you might enlist the help of an Analyst to help work up the background data and put it in accurate order. Then get a Pragmatist or Idealist to help you stay out of a "shoving it down his throat" selling stance.

Chapter 11

APPLYING THE METHODS: GETTING A FIX ON THAT DIFFICULT PERSON; COPING WITH YOUR BOSS AND WITH YOUR OWN DEFENSIVE BEHAVIOR

Those whom you experience as Difficult People will undoubtedly bring out the worst in you. They push your emotional buttons, threaten you, cause you distress, and generally propel you emotionally out of control. In so doing, they elicit from you whatever strategies you have learned to use when confronted by threat and conflict.

In this chapter, we look at managing defensive behavior, your own and your Difficult Person's. Then we look at how to cope in a particularly troublesome situation—when that Difficult Person who is driving you up the wall happens to be your boss. Finally, I've included an action plan for coping with a specific Difficult Person. To begin, let's examine defensive behavior as a set of strategies for getting out of trouble and how awareness of these strategies can help you cope.

DEFENSIVE BEHAVIOR

People react defensively to situations in which they feel both threatened and under pressure. The threat is not usually physical, although it might be, of course. In the workaday world, the blows we receive most frequently are psychological, and the deepest wounds we get from them are to our motivations and our feelings of self-worth.

We can be put under stress and feel tension at many different levels of our being. Most superficially, we can puzzle over a conflict of the moment—Should I go shopping now or wait 'til tomorrow?—decide to wait, and then feel a tinge of anxiety over a nagging doubt that the store will not be open the next day. At a deeper level, we may wonder if we've really included everything in that report we just delivered in haste to the boss. Here the stakes are higher, the possibility of exposure greater. More profound still is that anxiety we feel when we wonder, for instance, what it is that keeps us from being more successful—anxiety that touches the core of our being, the collection of needs, wants, and values that energizes all that we think and do. A flat attack at this level penetrates into the deepest source of feeling: the fear that we may be deprived of that which we cherish the most.

Let's say I'm a person for whom it's vital to feel needed and helpful to others. I proudly bring to you something I've worked long and hard on—a task. You, busy with other things, absentmindedly glance at it and put it to one side, perhaps with a mumbled "Oh, yeah, thanks." Whether it's a three-year project or a cake especially baked for the office party, you've poked a psychological finger in my vitals. Of course, you didn't mean it that way. You were so busy with your own work you didn't even notice that frozen, shocked look on my face. But intended or not, I will feel hurt, deflated, and unappreciated.

One sure effect will be the disruption of my ability to think, to plan clearly and rationally. If I'm not under pressure at the time, I will lick my wounds and, at length, begin to function normally again. Often, however, the time to recover is just not available. This is the case when the feeling of threat hits just when you're under pressure from others to do something. It is especially true when you've encountered opposition. Under these conditions— conflict or pressure on top of threat—we need strong countermeasures to keep from being overwhelmed. These countermeasures, consisting of a set of defensive strategies, learned early in life by every one of us, are designed to get us out of tight places, to avoid punishment, or somehow to disarm the opposition.

Strategies of Defense.

We each have our own unique ways of defending ourselves against threat, but there are some recognizable patterns. I have selected an example from family life to illustrate two of these defensive behavior patterns, because it is in that setting that they surface most clearly. In work settings, they are as potent but often covered with a facade of indirection and politeness.

Picture a family discussion about vacation plans for the summer. Twelve-year-old Brewster is making an enthusiastic and effective appeal for a family backpacking vacation. Suddenly older brother Tom interrupts and says, with disdain, "Look here, big man, when did you get so hot about backpacking? You can't even run around the track without panting like a sick hound." Silence. Then, "Oh, I dunno," says Brewster, face down, shoulders drooping. "I was reading about it—maybe nobody else wants to go."

Until that telling blow to his picture of himself as adventurous and competent, Brewster has used his active and creative mind well, arguing imaginatively for what he wanted. But creative, imaginative people often have strong needs to feel respected and admired by others. When Tom, with an unconscious feel for Brewster's jugular, struck, poor Brew faded away, abandoning the fight and caving in to the opposition. His response to the threat of lost respect was a typical Self-Blame→Give In defensive strategy.

To be fair to brother Tom, let's look at why he struck so hard at his cocky brother Brew. It was not just that Tom had a preference for a houseboating rather than a backpacking vacation, or even that Brewster claimed center stage, although both reasons may have been contributing factors. It was Brewster's last question that did it: "Don't you know how much it costs to rent a houseboat, Tom?" Whether he meant to or not, his tone of voice added, "You dummy." For Tom, who didn't have a ready answer and couldn't stand feeling dumb, the threat button had been pushed. His response, a feeling of suspicious anger together with an almost simultaneous attack, was typical of the Blame Others→Fight defensive strategy.

Everyone doesn't give in under fire like Brewster or charge like Tom, teeth bared and claws flying (recognize the Exploder from Chapter 2?). Other individuals in the same situation might have used one of two other rather common defensive strategies. Dig In→Withdraw and Distract→Make Nice.

Individuals using the Dig In→Withdraw strategy try to become immovable objects. They dig in, refusing to budge from a set position, denying any reality but their own. Eventually they withdraw from the situation into silence, sleep, a book, or a walk in the woods.

People using the strategy of Distract→Make Nice try to clown or sweeten their way out of trouble. If this had been Brewster's first line of defense, his response to Tom's sarcasm would have gone something like this: "Hey, Tommy, you're right. Remember how I almost fell on my face the last time we were out running? But I'm sure you can help us all get in shape for a good hike." Thick enough to cut with a knife? Sure, but remember you're not seeing the broad grin and clowning behavior that eases it into place.

We have all learned more than one way to cope with threatening situations. However, because of the way that defensive behavior is learned, most people tend to use one strategy at a time. If the first doesn't work, that is, if the threat and conflict don't go away, then a second strategy is brought to bear. Thus, if Tom had not let

Brewster give in, insisting that Brewster stay and be yelled at, Brewster might have begun to fight back. If that didn't work, at length he might have just gotten up and left the room.

It is important to realize that these defensive strategies are not initially consciously employed. As human beings we *must* try to give rational meaning to everything we do. Defensive behavior is no exception. Neither Tom nor Brewster saw themselves as caught up in automatic, deeply imprinted responses (psychologists call them signal reactions—the bullfighter waves his cape and we bulls charge). Yet the evidence is strong that we often respond emotionally to events before the exact nature of the events has registered in our consciousness. If you asked Tom why he blasted, he would accuse Brewster of unfair tactics or worse. Besides, he was only fighting for houseboating because it *was* the best vacation plan. However, witnesses to the "discussion" would have a much different view of what happened. They would be able to see Tom suddenly lean forward, his voice harsh and mean, finger jabbing at Brewster's chest. While those employing the Blame Others→Fight strategy always think they're fighting for the best alternative, we onlookers know that they're fighting for one purpose only—to get rid of the threat by getting rid of the opposition.

Before we leave them, three important points about defensive behavior in general should be made about surrendering Brewster and tough Tom. First, the more you know about what motivates a person, the more you know about what may threaten him or her. Brewster felt Tom's blow so painfully because for him being seen by others as bright and worthy of admiration was terribly important. Many people, however, have very little concern about how others judge them. They would not have been phased by Tom's remark.

Second, Brewster's behavior—giving in and going along—got him out of the emotional jam he was in. Tom stopped yelling at him, and he had time to pull himself together. "Ah, but he lost the argument," you say. True enough. In general, defensive strategies have the quality of getting you out of short-run trouble, but at some long-run cost.

Third, the social consequences to the family of this double set of defensive behaviors were mostly bad. Al-

though Brew's giving in stopped the fight, backpacking
may very well have been the best vacation for the family.
Because both Brew and Tom were put on the defensive,
no rational problem solving took place. The net result of
people pushing one another's threat buttons, whether at
home or in a work group, is an extraordinarily inefficient
use of the group's resources. All of these reasons make it
important to learn to cope with defensiveness in others
and in ourselves.

Coping with Defensive Behavior in Others.

The more you avoid inadvertently threatening others,
the less you will have to cope with their defensive, difficult behavior. In this case, an ounce of prevention is
indeed worth a pound of cure. Prevention, however, is
not an easy task. We all have secret sensitivities that we
keep hidden from others, even ourselves. Thus, sometimes
we have no choice but to try to remedy situations that
have already broken down.

Sweetening Sour Interactions. Think of yourself trying
to sell your boss on a change in office procedures. You've
been working hard, standing over him or her enthusiastically pointing out the advantages of the new system
over the old. Suddenly the boss speaks, hesitant, ac-
quiescing, not looking directly at you: "Well, I guess if
you folks really want to make these changes that much,
okay, I go along." Right in front of your eyes, in living
color, appears a Blame Self→Give In defensive response.
Somewhere in the meeting, out of your own interest and
enthusiasm, you may have said something that threatened.
Having recognized that a defensive strategy has intruded
into the situation, you now have a chance to do some
repairing—the sooner the better. Here's one possibility:
"Hold up, boss. These procedures we've been using for
the past three years must have been developed to deal
with some specific problems. Before we move ahead, can
we review what they were so that we don't end up solving
some new problems, but with the old ones back again?"
A true statement (or else don't say it), and one which
has the potential of gaining a less defensive response.
Especially if, this time, you shut up and listen carefully.
Possibly, you may find out that along with your terrific,
well-thought-out, factual presentation you were communi-
cating, "What idiot thought up these old procedures we've

been using?" Now you know who thought them up. That person sitting right in front of you.

Why not just let your boss surrender? Giving in would have gotten the boss out of a threat-conflict situation quite well, just the purpose for which it was learned. However, when you, the happy winner, had gone, the guilt and self-blaming would not have. Tomorrow you might well run into the boss's second line of defense, a resounding, "Forget it, Charlie!"

Managing Your Own Defensive Mode.

When your buttons have been pushed, as they are likely to be by those you find difficult, you will lose control. What you then do will be decided by your learned responses of long ago, rather than by the coping requirements of the present.

Here are some concrete steps to help you manage your own defensive mode.

Learn What You're Like. For the next month, keep an inner eye on yourself. When you are on the defensive, or shortly after, pay attention to how you behave, how you feel, and what you say. Your goal is to fix in your mind those behavioral signs that tell you when you are in the grip of your emergency mechanisms. Use the four defensive strategies we've just covered as a guide, but don't limit yourself to those.

Learn to Freeze Your Behavior. The moment you recognize that your defensive programming has taken over, stop what you're doing.

> EXAMPLE: Suddenly you become aware that you are walking toward your co-worker, finger jabbing the air, voice bouncing off the walls, stomach clamped tight. Stop where you are, mumble something, shut up, and sit down. (Don't worry about the silence, someone will find it.)
>
> EXAMPLE: You are on the phone, the PTA president is saying, "I've had so much trouble finding someone to take over as treasurer, and you've always been so good *in the past* about picking up these things." You hear yourself saying, "Well, if you really can't get anyone else, I guess . . ." You feel that tug on you to be a good kid or else you won't be appreciated. These are your cues to interrupt yourself and say, "Wait a minute, I need to think about this. I'll call you back in five minutes." Clunk, you hang up the phone.

Cutting off the interaction abruptly like this may seem rather drastic, but there are good reasons for doing so. First, you're trying to manage your behavior just at the time that it's most difficult to manage. The surest way is to simply stop it. Second, to refine and modify what you're doing while in the midst of an overlearned and heavily reinforced learning sequence requires extraordinary control. Remember that people don't plan to be defensive, it just pops out of them. You become aware after the toboggan is partway down the slide, too scared, steamed, or guilty for anything but the brakes.

By interrupting the interaction you give yourself a chance to compose yourself and think about what's happening. In the interval, look at yourself from the outside. Isn't it just fascinating that, having previously decided to cut down on your volunteer work (you're already on four committees, and doing a lousy job because you're spread so thin), you almost said yes to another assignment? Recognize in yourself a wonderful collection of all kinds of intentions, productive and powerful thinking strategies, and some pretty interesting crazinesses. Those times when you do find yourself pulled and pushed from within and without, even a wisp of an "Am I not interesting?" thought can do wonders for your perspective.

Try to Find the Threat. Something happened to you just before you started to charge, give in, clown around, or whatever you do when you're defensive. Try to identify what it was. It is often impossible to do. In most social and work settings the threats that hit us are masked, subtle, often unintentional. They touch upon secret and unreal fears that others could not know about.

I am acutely aware of such a secret sensitivity in my own professional life. I will be talking with clients or colleagues when one of them will say, "I ran into John Jones the other day; he's a consultant like you, you know. He was really great. Very helpful." After years of it, I am now prepared for the abdominal twinge I will feel just at the level of my diaphragm. Now, why should I find a compliment to a fellow consultant a threat when, often, I know John Jones myself, and even *I* think he's competent? My guess is that I inwardly add to the comment "and he's better than you." Just the kind of suspicious worry that you'd expect from someone who likes to be admired by others as much as I do.

The more knowledge you have of the things that threaten you, the more you can anticipate your reaction and be ready with a more productive response. For instance, I have taught myself to say, "That's great" when "John Jones" is mentioned favorably to me. It buys time for me to think respectfully of the tenacity with which my "crazy" reactions hang on.

An Exercise to Help. I suggest this brief exercise as a help in strengthening your awareness of your own ways of being defensive. Take a plain sheet of paper and fold it lengthwise. On one side of the paper list words and phrases that describe what you do and how you feel when you are in your defensive mode. Does your voice get loud, harsh, accusing? Do you feel suddenly frightened or anxious about whether someone (anyone) accepts you, approves of you, likes you? Do you suddenly feel irritated or bored in a meeting and want to get out? Do you repeat the same arguments over and over again regardless of what's been said by others?

On the other half of your paper jot down as many situations as you can that appear threatening to you. A group of friends who go to coffee without inviting you? Your gem of wisdom ignored by the members of your group? Work returned to you with a "you didn't do it right, stupid" message, whether intended or not? You may think the list will be endless but most people find that it's variations of five incidents happening over and over.

It helps to review your list with individuals who know you well *and* who will be candid. I suggest that you give them specific permission to tell you what you don't want to hear. Be suspicious if it's all nice. Also, be prepared to avoid explaining away the first behaviors they point out, or they'll also be the last. There are always "reasons" for everything. The reasons only describe what the situational factors were, not why you started yelling.

COPING WITH THE BOSS

Coping with Difficult People is hardly ever easy. When your Difficult Person also happens to be your boss, the hurdles automatically increase in size. Not that either your boss or you becomes more implicitly difficult. Only that now there are added situational factors that require attention and increase the likelihood that you and your boss will react defensively.

Bosses have power, or at least subordinates think they do. Knowing this and fearing the worst, most of us hold off on coping with bosses until we can't stand it any more. At that point, the interaction has probably become so mired in pent-up emotions that what was intended as coping rapidly slides into killing, quitting, or copping out.

A better approach is to start coping as soon as possible, but with reasonable caution. A slow, positive beginning gives you a chance to test the waters and discover the degree to which *your* boss is amenable to change. Here are some important things to remember.

They Know Not What They Do.

Most of us are only partly aware of the impact we have on others. Bosses suffer from this comfortable failing even more than the rest of us, especially white-collar bosses in middle- and higher-management levels. I have listened incredulously to otherwise knowledgeable executives say: "Why I'm just good old Dave. How can anyone be afraid to tell me anything?" To Dave, shouting at people and insulting them are just things he does when he's sore. The suppressed anger of his subordinates, resentful at being called down like children, is kept secret from him. Dave suffers from the curse of the powerful—being cut off from feedback about the unplanned effects of what they do. Concerned primarily with whether or not his plans were carried out, he simply doesn't think to ask about any other possible consequence of the blizzards he blows.

Intentions Are an Entry.

While the road to hell *may* be paved with good intentions, there is a difference between a person who is purposely trying to hurt you and one who does it unthinkingly. With the former, there's nothing to do but assess your own resources, use the coping methods as boldly as you can, and force the hostility into the open.

When others' *intentions* are benevolent, however, you have some leverage. You can point out that their actions have had results they didn't intend. Here's the dialogue:

YOU: Dave, I asked for this appointment to talk about something a little different. When I went back to my desk yesterday, I was feeling a little low and so I did some thinking. The fact is, when I sit in your office while you're on the phone talking to someone for ten minutes, I feel like I'm wasting my time. Is there some way we could avoid that?

By making an appointment with your boss you indicate that you, and what you want to talk about, are important. Shun "my door is open all the time" situations for any but casual or social conversations.

DAVE (rising in anger): Now wait a minute. I only take important calls—that was Rogers, President of Peters Company . . .

YOU (interrupting): Wait a minute, Dave. I know they're important, just like I know you're the boss. I *didn't* know whether you knew that I was getting antsy about other things I could be doing.

You were ready with "I know you're the boss" because you had figured Dave as someone with a high control orientation—people like this get riled when they feel nibbles on their authority.

DAVE: Well, no, I hadn't thought about it that way. When old Rogers calls, I answer. He's our biggest customer.

YOU: Right. And you should answer. How about my interrupting to ask if I can go back to my office until you're through?

You thought of this possible solution in advance, knowing that tension in the boss's office might interfere with your thinking.

DAVE: Of course. You know you can always do anything that helps the business.

And "good old Dave" really believes it.

Remember, They Look Bigger from Below.

People tend to attribute to those of higher status considerably more power than high level people believe they have. The behavioral results of this difference in perception all work against open communication. It's hard for an employee who clearly and repeatedly informs management about a problem not to feel disappointment, or at least disenchantment, when nothing visible happens. Upper management, in turn, may have taken relevant, if only partially effective, action, but they are likely to forget to inform the complainers. The unspoken dialogue goes something like this: "I've told you about it, you haven't fixed it, therefore you must not care."/"Don't they know that we always do everything we can to solve problems. Everyone should realize that we do. Do we have to tell them specifically about everything?" Here are two action conclusions that can help to redress this unhappy state of affairs.

Ask About What Happened. It pays to follow up any complaint or suggestion with an inquiry about what's happened. This demonstrates your interest and keeps the matter in the active file, but it also lowers your frustration level, and this helps you keep from feeling bad about yourself. Sure, they should let you know about it without your asking, but it's your tension that needs to be relieved.

Counsel Your Boss When Possible. Particularly if your approach to things is different from that of your boss, be alert for opportunities to take a counseling role. You can help keep him or her—and therefore you—out of trouble with questions like, "How are you making out with so and so these days?" (This individual could be the big boss, or perhaps a peer of your boss who's been a problem.) Having thrown out that question you can set yourself to listen and perhaps toss out more problem-solving questions. But be careful not to sympathize, lecture, join in a mutual "ain't it awful" conversation, or do any of the other things friends do to keep each other from solving problems.

Keep Ahead of the Game.

If your boss's approach to life is aggressive—that is, quick acting, positive, confident—do anything you can to be responsive. When you receive an order or request, send back an outline of what you'll do and by when. If problems arise, give interim reports on what you're doing, or plan to do, before the boss asks. Keep aggressive bosses *informed* of your plans and actions, but don't ask them for approval, directly or by hesitation, unless your projected plan is clearly *not* part of your delegated responsibilities.

Aggressive, well-informed people who are confident in their own opinions are usually very forceful speakers and arguers. They can also turn a productive problem-solving discussion into group-think and hardly know it. From the observer's point it looks this way:

JOE: Look at that trend line. If we don't change our pricing structure, we're going to end up selling a million seven-cent paper clips for six cents and go broke.

SAM: No sir! We've contained our costs this year and at the old price we'll pull sales away from all our competitors. What's the point of cost cutting if we don't use it?

MARY (the boss, shoving the paperwork away, as if the discussion were over): Well, I believe Joe's got a good point. Sales without profit we've had enough of.

SAM (slight hesitation): Okay, then. I'll prepare tentative price lists for a final approval next week.

MARY (slightly puzzled): I guess that means we all agree—let's go to it.

I have seen such a perfunctory nondecision process occur many times. The discussion subtly changes from "What's the best solution?" to "How can we do what the boss wants, dumb as it sounds." An equally frustrating phenomenon occurs in a two-person discussion when the boss's "I think we should do it this way" is interpreted as a decision, rather than opinion.

Your coping reply should be to ask "Is that a decision or just your opinion at this stage?" (Unless, of course, the boss has selected the best alternative—yours, naturally.)

Plan Ahead for Directness.

The added stresses of the authority relationship make it valuable to plan ahead when coping with the boss. Thinking through the best way to put something is not, in itself, devious. In fact, it helps to be candid and direct if you've assured yourself that the words you use will not in themselves threaten your boss. Think about the kind of person he or she is, what his or her important motivations are, what coping steps might be needed. This can help reduce unfortunate surprises and keep you from being over- or under-assertive.

DEVELOPING A COPING PLAN

At times you will be faced with the necessity of coping with a *very* Difficult Person, perhaps your boss or someone else with whom you've had a long and perilous relationship. In these cases, thinking through what needs to be done, and how you're going to do it, is well worthwhile. On the next few pages is a Coping Analysis Form—a series of questions that have helped my clients develop an effective coping plan. I suggest you carefully follow the procedure below in using it, particularly when you anticipate a hard time coping:

Complete the questions as thoughtfully and honestly as you can.

Review the plan with someone with whom you can be candid and who will be direct with you.

Reread those portions of the book most pertinent to the Difficult Person you have in mind. Remember that some individuals are actually combinations of the Difficult Person types described here. You may, for example, have to use coping steps suitable for both Snipers and Super-Agreeables in coping with your troublesome other. After you have smoked out the intention to hurt in those quips at your expense, you might quickly show some personal interest in your Sniping Super-Agreeable. Thus, your coping plan would include "invite her to coffee" as well as "don't let those slurs go by."

If you determine that you need practice in standing up to another or asking questions without sounding like a district attorney, by all means get it. If possible, get someone to role play your Difficult Person. If that's not feasible, use a mirror. Do the practicing out loud, not just in your mind. Internal conversations tend to take on an air of fantasy. Besides, if you don't hear yourself until you're in action, you may panic, especially if you're trying an approach new for you.

Make your action plan realistic so that you can hold yourself to it.

DIFFICULT PERSON COPING PLAN

1. Describe in as much detail as possible the behavior of a person you find to be difficult.
2. Write down briefly your understanding of that behavior.
3. Think now of your own past behavior as you have interacted with that person. Describe it in as much detail as you can. Are there times and/or situations when the interaction seems better? Worse?
4. Now think of the coping behaviors most likely to be useful with the Difficult Person you have described. Consider that some behavior represents a mixture of defensive reactions. What have you tried that seemed to work? What has not worked?
5. As you review what you have written down under item 3, what do you see in yourself that requires acknowledgment and attention to enable you to best carry out the most promising coping behavior?
6. With which coping behaviors do you need skill practice?
7. Action plan: What will you do, by what date?

THE CONFIDENCE TO COPE

Now you've completed your plan, thought through a workable strategy, and defined some action steps. All that remains is the action—dry mouth, thumping heart, sweaty palms and all. Can I really carry it off? Will it be a disaster? Will I look like a fool? I have had thoughts like these expressed to me by mature, experienced executives thinking ahead to an unpleasant encounter with an impossible person. I am sure that is why nothing gives me more professional satisfaction than hearing the following remark from a client: "I want to tell you about my last brush with so and so. I tried the coping methods and they worked." There are seldom any miracles, but there are very real changes in the way the interaction went. I have also seen that the confidence to cope does not arise magically. In fact, it is that magical wish that those Difficult People were different than they actually are that leads to bitter passivity and resentment. Rather, confidence arises from these staunch friends: acknowledgment of your own feelings; a vision of success; and a little "toe dipping" practice.

Cherish an awareness that coping with Difficult People is *never* easy and hardly ever fun. If you know what you're doing, you ought to feel uneasy. Acknowledgment of fear is the first step toward moving beyond it.

Try to build a vision of how the encounter would go if everything worked well. Include in your vision a sequence in which you get into trouble while coping and then get out of it. The evidence is substantial that this anticipation of success can help to pull you along past self-doubts, uncertainty, or unforeseen problems.

Increase your confidence in the power of the coping methods themselves by trying them out in low-risk situations. Test out the power of standing up to, but not fighting with, that loudmouth in your car pool. The next time he (or she) says "That's a dumb idea," plant a firm and loud "I disagree" right in the middle of the painful silence and watch what happens. The next time modify your approach. Amplify the volume, pull back a little or add an "In my opinion it's a good idea." You will gain in sureness as you see, first, that you've survived the experience, and, second, that the loudmouth now pays more attention to you and what you say.

Finally, let your confidence to cope rest securely on the knowledge that many people just like you have found that coping effectively with difficult people is possible. Like a cold shower, it may be awful in anticipation, but it feels great when it's over.

REFERENCES

Anderson, Carl R. "Locus of Control, Coping Behavior and Performance." *Journal of Applied Psychology*, 66, 4, 1977, pp. 446–51.

Bramson, Robert M. "The Effects of Group Training on Social Sensitivity." Doctoral dissertation, University of California, Berkeley, 1969.

Carson, Robert D. *Interaction Concepts of Personality*. Chicago: Aldine, 1969.

Church, Joseph. *Language and the Discovery of Reality*. New York: Random House (Vintage Books), 1961.

Churchman, C. West. *The Design of Inquiring Systems*. New York: Basic Books, 1971.

Corey, G. *I Never Knew I Had a Chance*. Monterey, Calif.: Brooks/Cole, 1978.

Doyle, Michael, and David Strauss. *How to Make Meetings Work*. Chicago: Playboy Press, 1976.

Erikson, Erik H. *Toys and Reasons*. New York: Norton, 1977.

Fagen, Stanley A., Nicholas J. Long, and Donald Stevens. *Teaching Children Self-control*. Columbus, Ohio: Merrill, 1975.

Fromm, Erich. *Man For Himself: An Inquiry into the Psychology of Ethics*. Greenwich, N.Y.: Fawcett, 1947.

Hough, Richard. *Captain Bligh and Mr. Christian*. New York: Dutton, 1973.

Kantor, David, and William Lehr. *Inside the Family*. San Francisco: Jossey-Bass, 1975.

Klein, George S. *Perception, Motives and Personality*. New York: Knopf, 1970.

Lazarus, R. S. *Psychological Stress and the Coping Process*. New York: McGraw-Hill, 1966.

Lederer, William J., and Don D. Jackson. *The Mirages of Marriage*. New York: Norton, 1968.

Leeper, R. "Some Needed Developments in the Motivated Theory of Emotions." *Nebraska Symposium on Motivation*, 13, 1965, pp. 25–122.

Maher, Bredan. *Clinical Psychology and Personality: The Selected Papers of George Kelly*. New York: Wiley, 1969, pp. 267–80.

McGee, P., and V. Grandall. "Belief in Internal-External Control of Reinforcements and Academic Performance." *Child Development*, 1968, pp. 91–102.

Rotter, J. B. "Generalized Expectancies for Internal Versus External Control of Reinforcement." *Psychological Monographs*, 80, 1966, pp. 1–28.

Satir, Virginia. *Conjoint Family Therapy*, rev. ed. Palo Alto, Calif.: Science and Behavioral Books, 1967.

————. *People Making*. Palo Alto, Calif.: Science and Behavorial Books, 1972.

Snow, C. P. *Variety of Men*. New York: Scribner, 1966.

Tock, Hans H. *Violent Men*. Chicago: Aldine, 1969.

Watson, D., and R. Thorp. *Self-directed Behavior: Self-modification for Personal Adjustment*. Monterey, Calif.: Brooks/Cole, 1977.

Watzlawick, P., Janet H. Beavin, and D. D. Jackson. *Pragmatics of Human Communication: A Study of Interactional Patterns, Pathologies and Paradoxes*. New York: Norton, 1967.

Williams, R., and J. Long. *Toward a Self-managed Lifestyle*. Boston: Houghton Mifflin, 1975.

INDEX